Arizona's Mountains

Arizona's Mountains

A Hiking and Climbing Guide

Bob and Dotty Martin

CORDILLERA PRESS, INC.

Publishers in the Rockies

Library of Congress Cataloging-in-Publication Data

Martin, Bob, 1920-
    Arizona's mountains.

    Includes index.
    1. Hiking — Arizona — Guide-books.
    2. Rock climbing — Arizona — Guide-books.
    3. Arizona — Description and travel — 1951-   — Guide-books.
I. Martin, Dotty, 1921-   II. Title.
GV199.42.A7M37   917.91'0433   87-15518
ISBN 0-917895-18-5

Printed in the United States of America

    First Edition

    1 2 3 4 5 6 7 8 9

Back cover photograph courtesy of John Morgan.
Front cover and all other photographs courtesy of the authors.

Book Design & Typography —
    Richard M. Kohen, Shadow Canyon Graphics, Evergreen, Colorado

Cordillera Press, Inc.
Post Office Box 3699
Evergreen, Colorado 80439

Contents

.

.

Area Map

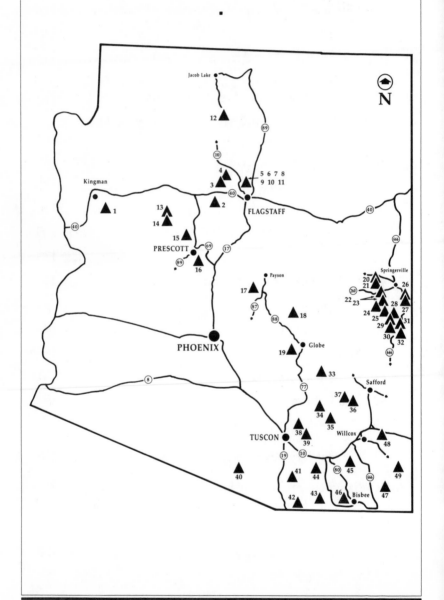

Introduction
Using This Guide

.

The Arizona mountains provide varied experiences for sightseers, hikers, and climbers of all levels of ability. Some of the summits described in this book can be visited by backroad automobile drives. Other summits can be climbed by short easy walks. Still other summits require long hikes on trail in wilderness areas. Some hikes take skills of navigation and route finding. Others are exhausting bushwhacks. Finally, there is at least one ascent that takes technical climbing skills. So regardless of your interests or ability, you should find some Arizona high summits worthy of a visit.

Unlike the great mountain ranges of some other western states, the Arizona mountains rise abruptly as isolated high areas. The general elevation of much of the northern portion of the state is above six thousand feet, and the summits rise to high points above twelve thousand feet at San Francisco Mountain. The second highest area is in the White Mountains of eastern Arizona. The general terrain of the White Mountains is above eight thousand feet, and the highest mountain there exceeds eleven thousand feet.

In southeastern Arizona, the deserts are only a few thousand feet in elevation and the highest mountains exceed ten thousand feet. Consequently, the elevation gain for many of the southeastern summits is greater than for the summits in the northern part of the state. From a hiking and climbing standpoint, the northern summits are easier to reach since most of the hiking is through forested areas. In the southeast, the mountains are more rocky and their lower slopes are covered with desert vegetation that often makes off-trail hiking difficult.

The Arizona mountains offer a variety of hiking and climbing probably unmatched by any other state. Arizona's highest summits, those over twelve thousand feet, offer truly alpine conditions. Vast forested areas and grassy meadows provide much fine hiking, both on trails and on off-trail routes. Many desert ranges provide diverse hiking experiences. These include trail walking, easy off-trail hiking, desert bushwhacking, rock scrambling, and technical climbing.

Unlike mountain climbing in many states, visiting Arizona's high summits can be a year round activity. There are ample opportunities for warm desert hiking in the winter as well as for cool high-altitude hiking in the summer.

When we decided to write about Arizona's highest summits, we needed a list of the highest peaks in the state. We listed well over a hundred Arizona summits higher than nine thousand feet. Some of these high summits are on Indian Reservations. Many of these mountains are off limits to hikers or their access is questionable. Because of the problem of access, we decided that the mountains on the Indian Reservations are not good climbing objectives for the average hiker.

After eliminating the peaks on Indian Reservations from the list of summits above nine thousand feet, eighty-four summits remained. These are listed in Appendix One and make a reasonable climbing goal.

Now a word on how we define a summit. Our standard is the generally accepted definition that a summit is a point that rises at least three hundred feet above all saddles that lead from it to higher peaks. Thus, if you were coming along any ridge from a higher point, you would have to climb at least three hundred feet to reach the summit. Summits are sometimes referred to as "separate summits" or "ranked summits." In Appendix One, these summits are ranked in order of elevation. Sixty-six of the summits listed in Appendix 1 are ranked.

In addition to the ranked summits, there are other high points that are named, but which do not qualify as separate summits. These named high points do not rise three hundred feet above a saddle leading to a higher peak. The named high points are listed in Appendix 1 according to their elevation, but are not ranked. Nevertheless, we consider the named high points to be worthy climbing objectives.

In addition to the summits nine thousand feet and above, there are many fine hikes to the high points of mountain ranges that don't reach the nine-thousand-foot level. We have included hikes to the high points of nineteen ranges between seven thousand and nine thousand feet. They are listed in Appendix Two.

As a matter of information, summits above nine thousand feet on Indian Reservations are shown in Appendix Three.

This guide contains route descriptions to 103 mountains — all eighty-four of the peaks nine thousand feet and above, plus the nineteen high points of ranges that are between seven thousand and nine thousand feet. Surprisingly, from a hiking and climbing standpoint, all of the summits above nine thousand feet are within the capabilities of most hikers. Many are easy walks and some can be visited by automobile. The hardest non-trail hikes are only moderate bushwhacks or rock scrambles.

The eighty-four mountains nine thousand feet and above can be reached as follows:

    10 by automobile drives
    50 by short trail or easy off-trail hikes, a half

day or less
15 by longer trail or easy off-trail hikes, one day
  or less
9 by moderate off-trail hikes, one day or less

Some of the nineteen high points of ranges between seven and nine thousand feet are harder to climb than any of the summits above nine thousand feet. The nineteen high points of ranges between seven and nine thousand feet can be reached as follows:
3 by automobile drives
2 by trail or easy off-trail, half day hikes
3 by trail or easy off-trail, day hikes
1 by trail, extremely long day hike or backpack
5 by moderate or harder off-trail, day hikes
5 by difficult day hikes, including one with
  technical climbing

Some of the routes to "mountains" described in this book may seem laughingly short to many experienced mountaineers and long-distance hikers. We thought so too when we started out to climb them all. As we got along, though, we found there was great pleasure in making several of these short hikes in a day's outing.
The 103 summits covered by the route descriptions are grouped into forty-nine chapters, each chapter including enough hiking to make a reasonable day's outing. The area covered by these hikes extends some four hundred miles, from the Chiricahua Mountains in the southeastern part of Arizona to the Hualapai Mountains in the northwest. Covering all of this territory, in addition to the hiking, will give you a good look at much of the state of Arizona.
Most of the hikes described and the summits visited are on National Forest lands and are open to hikers. Similarly, lands controlled by the Bureau of Land Management (BLM) and the National Park Service are

open to hikers. Arizona state lands are another matter,
as they are not open on an unrestricted basis to the
people who own them. There is a permit system which
is used for controlling access to state lands. Generally,
a hunting or fishing license permits access to state
lands. Hiking on private lands should be avoided
except with permission of the landowner. We have
found that ranchers are usually cooperative in allowing
hiking on their lands when permission is requested.

One problem is identifying the ownership of the
lands. There are several hikes in this book where
access could be a problem and they are included only
because they get you to a high point objective. We
have tried to describe thoroughly the access problems
on such hikes, but bear in mind that conditions change
and that new owners, new policies, new roads, and
any number of other factors can make the situation
different than it was when we were there.

At the beginning of each chapter, tabular material
gives pertinent information about each hike. The
General description briefly summarizes the character of
the hike. **Hiking distance** is the approximate round-trip
distance from the designated starting point. **Starting
elevation** is the elevation at the indicated parking
place. **High points** are the highest elevations reached
on the hikes. **Elevation gain** is the total amount of
climbing required on the hike. In many cases the
elevation gain is greater than the difference between
the starting elevation and the high point because of
descents along the ascent route. Where there is more
than one hike in a chapter, hiking distance, starting
elevation, high points, and elevation gains are shown
as a range. Specifics for each hike are included in the
descriptions. **Maps** are the latest U.S.G.S. topographic
map quadrangles and National Forest maps that cover
the area of the hikes. Where available, the newer 7.5
minute U.S.G.S. topographic maps are listed both

in the hike description and in the appendices.

Along with an Arizona state highway map, the National Forest maps are essential in getting to the starting point for many hikes. The U.S.G.S. topographic map quadrangles would not be needed on most hikes, but we consider them essential on some of the more involved hikes and in such cases they are marked "essential." Unfortunately, some of the areas are only covered by the older 15 minute U.S.G.S. quadrangles, and these are out of date in many respects. The topography hasn't changed, however, so even the old maps often will be helpful.

This guide is intended to list the high summits of Arizona and tell you how to get to them. It is not intended to tell you how to hike, how to prepare for a hike, what to take, or when to go. If you are not an experienced hiker, you will want to join a hiking club, hike with experienced companions, and read some of the many books that can help prepare you for safe hiking.

We have described each hike to the best of our ability, *but we can take no responsibility for your using the information in a safe manner. This guide is not a substitute for your experience and common sense.* There may be errors in the route descriptions because changes may have been made in roads and trails. Weather conditions may be greatly different when you are there than they were when we took these hikes. Always be well prepared and don't overextend yourself on any hike. After all, these mountains will still be there for you to come back another time. We hope you take ample precautions and have many enjoyable hours of driving and hiking the routes we have described.

We have made most of these hikes together. Since we began spending our winters in Arizona, the Southern Arizona Hiking Club has provided us with much useful hiking information, as well as fellowship and good times. Those who have gone on one or more of the hikes with us, or who have provided information, include Mike Coltrin, Don Eve, Eber Glendenning, Gilbert Jimenez, Doug Kasian, Marcille Lynn, John Peterson, Dave Shope, Thom Wade, and Tom Wentzel. We have enjoyed their companionship and appreciate all of the help they and others have given us.

■

Classification of Hikes

.

T he "Classification of Hikes" table is intended to help you select hikes that are of the most interest to you and that best fit your hiking ability. The duration of the hike is indicated by the categories down the left side of the page. The difficulty is indicated across the top. If hikes of different types are included in a chapter, that chapter number is shown in more than one box. The duration is intended to be for the average or slow hiker. The difficulty reflects the hardest portion of the hike. Often the difficulty of a hike can be reduced by omitting a portion of the climb. Thus, many fine hikes can be made that do not take you all the way to the summit.

The categories across the top of the page show the type of footing encountered on the hike. **Trail** hikes are on trails, old roads, or on well-beaten paths. **Easy off-trail** hikes are across meadows or through open forests. Climbing steep slopes, rock-hopping in canyons, and easy bushwhacking through scattered vegetation or timbered areas constitute **Moderate off-trail** hikes. **Harder off-trail** hikes involve rock scrambling and harder bushwhacking. The **Most difficult or technical** trips require difficult rock scrambling and rugged bushwhacking, steep rock climbing with some exposure, or use of technical climbing equipment.

For the duration of the hikes indicated on the left side of the table, we consider **Half day** hikes to be five hours or less, **Short day** hikes to be six to eight hours, and **Long day** hikes to take nine hours or more. The duration is for each individual hike and does not include time to drive to and from the starting point.

.

	Trail	Easy off-trail	Moderate off-trail	Harder off-trail	Most difficult or technical
Two hours or less	22 36	5 9 11 12 20 21 22 23 25 26 28 29 30 31 36 37	18 23 25 28 37		
Half day	14 32	23 29 30	46		
Short day	4 13 43	5 8 42	1 3 27 47	15	48
Long day	6 24 34 39 41 43 49	6 41 49	7 49	10 17 45	33 40 35 44

Drives — 2   11   16   18   19   21   25   31   36   37   38

Northern Ranges

.

T he northern area includes the highest summits of
Arizona, the only peaks in the state that rise
above twelve thousand feet. San Francisco Mountain,
north of Flagstaff, encompasses the six highest points
in the state. Humphreys Peak, at 12,633 feet, is the
high point of Arizona. Its neighbor, Agassiz Peak, at
12,356 feet, is the second highest. Two other peaks,
Fremont Peak and Doyle Peak, are on the ridge
extending east from Agassiz Peak. Two named ridge
points, Aubineau Peak and Rees Peak, are on the
ridge east of Humphreys Peak. These six summits
surround an area known as the "Inner Basin."

There is some confusion in terminology for the
mountains in the Flagstaff area. While "San Francisco
Mountain" is the official name of the group of high
summits, these mountains are more commonly
referred to as the "San Francisco Peaks." The high
portion of San Francisco Mountain is designated as
the "San Francisco Peaks Natural Area."

Other summits rise from the high plateau somewhat
isolated from San Francisco Mountain. Although not
nearly as high, such mountains as Kendrick Peak,
Hochderffer Hills, Sitgreaves Mountain, and Bill
Williams Mountain dominate their areas. Farther
west, the Hualapai Mountains near Kingman rise in
bold relief from a much lower base.

North of the Grand Canyon, the Kaibab Plateau is
a vast area of high ground. Two "summits" above
nine thousand feet on the Kaibab Plateau are as high
as some of the summits surrounding San Francisco
Mountain, but they rise only slightly from the

surrounding terrain.

The northeastern part of Arizona is within the Navajo Indian Reservation. Several mountain ranges on the reservation in the extreme northeastern corner of the state exceed nine thousand feet.

■

1

Hualapai Peak

Trail in Hualapai Mountain Park.

General description: A varied hike on excellent scenic trails and steep eroded roads, with a final short bushwhack and rock scramble

Hiking distance: 8 miles

Starting elevation: 6,814 feet

High point: 8,417 feet

Elevation gain: 2,200 feet

Maps: 7.5 minute Hualapai Peak;
Hualapai Mountain Park Trail System (essential)

.

T he Hualapai Mountains form an isolated high
mountain range in the northwestern part of
Arizona. Hualapai Peak, at 8,417 feet, is the high point.
The Hualapai Mountain Park, a Mohave County Parks
Department facility, is the starting point for a climb of
Hualapai Peak.

At the time of our visit in October 1986, Hualapai
Peak was not easily accessible, requiring a hike up
steep eroded roads, bushwhacking, and rock scrambling. You may be fortunate, however, since the Parks
Department has plans to extend its trail system with a
trail going to the top of Hualapai Peak. Therefore, it is
essential to stop at the park ranger station both to get
a map of the trail system and to find out if there is a
better way to get to Hualapai Peak than the one
described here. The following description covers the
best route at the time of our visit.

At Kingman, take exit 51 south off of Interstate 40.
Follow Stockton Hill Road south, which becomes
Hualapai Mountain Road at Andy Devine Avenue
(Business Interstate 40). Continue eleven miles to the
Hualapai Mountain Park ranger station on the right
side of the road. Pick up a trail map and get the latest
information on the status of the trail system.

Drive two-tenths of a mile beyond the ranger station
to a junction. Turn right toward a cabin area. Follow a
narrow paved road and then a steep rutted dirt road
three-quarters of a mile to a trailhead. There is limited
parking on the right side of the road in front of a
locked gate.

Hike up the Aspen Springs Trail. This excellent
well-marked trail winds around and between huge
boulders as it makes its way through the forest. After

Looking north to Hayden Peak from Hualapai Peak.

almost a mile, take the left fork and follow the Potato Patch Loop Trail. This trail circles high on the east side of Aspen Peak and offers spectacular views of the valley below. As the trail descends somewhat on the south side of Aspen Peak it meets a service road. This dirt road leads to some communications equipment near the top of Hualapai Peak.

Turn left and hike along the service road as it crosses a valley and then climbs steeply up the south side of Hualapai Peak. The steep, rutted, dirt and gravel road is really miserable for hiking, but it gets you to within a hundred vertical feet of the summit. At the end of the road you are south of some cliffs that are above and behind the communications facilities. Along the road you come to a locked gate with a sign "No Admittance." The park ranger assured us that this applies only to vehicles and that hiking is permitted anywhere in the area.

From the end of the road, the climb to the summit is a short but steep bushwhack and rock scramble. There appears to be no best way to go, but there has been a good bit of foot traffic to the right of the cliffs. The highest summit rock with its benchmark is best climbed from the east.

The views from this 8,417-foot isolated mountaintop are unobstructed. Only air pollution limits the distance you can see in any direction.

Hualapai Mountain Park is well worth a visit even if you don't climb Hualapai Peak. Its well-planned trails offer a variety of potential hikes to fit the desires of almost any hiker. The altitude and corresponding change in vegetation make this mountain park truly an "island in the desert."

■

2

Bill Williams Mountain

.

General description: A drive to a summit with excellent
   view points along the way
Hiking distance: Optional
High point: 9,256 feet
Maps: 15 minute Bill Williams Mountain;
   Kaibab National Forest

.

B ill Williams Mountain is an isolated summit west of
   Flagstaff that overlooks the town of Williams. A
road leads to the top, where communications equipment is located. Bill Williams Mountain is the most
westerly of the Arizona summits above nine thousand
feet and shouldn't be confused with the Bill Williams
Mountains, a low range just east of Lake Havasu.

   Access is from forest road 173 that runs south from
Williams. Five miles south of Williams, turn west from
forest road 173 onto road 111. Drive west on road 111
as it winds its way up the mountain to the summit.
   There are numerous scenic views, including some
spectacular views of jagged rock pinnacles, that are
worth stops on the way to the summit. The high point
at 9,256 feet affords a panoramic look and lets you feel
the isolation of this mountain.

■

Peak 9,004
and Sitgreaves Mountain

San Francisco Mountain from the summit of Sitgreaves Mountain.

■

General description: A hike through timber with
route-finding required
Hiking distance: 8 miles
Starting elevation: 7,600 feet
High points: 9,004 and 9,388 feet
Elevation gain: 2,400 feet
Maps: 15 minute Williams (essential);
7.5 minute Parks (essential);
Kaibab National Forest

■

S itgreaves Mountain is a broad-based, forested
mountain which stands alone in the area west of
Flagstaff and north of Interstate 40. It rises over two
thousand feet above the surrounding flat country. Peak
9,004 is a separate summit on the eastern flank of
Sitgreaves Mountain. The two summits can be combined on a moderate hike through timbered lands. This
off-trail hike takes some navigational skills, both for the
climb and to find your way back to the starting point.

From exit 171 on Interstate 40 west of Flagstaff, drive
north on forest road 74 (passing a compressor station
on the left after about one mile) for five miles to a
junction with forest road 75. Turn right on road 75 and
drive two miles east and south to a junction with road
794. Make a sharp left turn on road 794 and drive
northeast a half mile. Park near a sharp turn to the
south.

The first objective is peak 9,004, which is northeast
of the starting point. From the initial elevation of 7,600
feet, the climb of fourteen-hundred vertical feet covers
a two-mile distance. The key to Peak 9,004 is its
southwest ridge. Start by heading east and northeast to
get into a major drainage. Follow this drainage for
perhaps a quarter-mile and then climb to the ridge on
your right. You should reach the ridge crest at about
8,200 feet.

Hike steeply northeast up the ridge for four-hundred
vertical feet to a ridge point at 8,625 feet, where the
ridge becomes decidedly more gradual. Continue
northeast over a couple of minor ridge points and then
through a steep meadow. This area offers the only
distant views from the ridge. Continue beyond the
meadow to the summit of Peak 9,004.

Although the views are quite restricted, the summit of Peak 9,004 is apparent as there are sharp drop-offs in all directions. Sitgreaves Mountain is northwest of Peak 9,004 and a little over a mile away, but there are several obstacles along the route between the two peaks. First, descend northwest and then bear a little left to get to an 8,630-foot saddle on the ridge toward Sitgreaves Mountain.

The next problem is to get around a rather sharp 8,730-foot ridge point. We bypassed this ridge point on the right, but it may be better to skirt it on the left or climb over it. Once around the ridge point, you are in an 8,610-foot saddle, the low point between Peak 9,004 and Sitgreaves Mountain.

Next, climb steeply northwest through the forest to a flat 8,990-foot ridge point. Descend through another saddle and continue northwest through a broad grassy meadow to a 9,290-foot high point. This point offers good views to the south and you can see the summit of Sitgreaves Mountain only a little higher to the northwest. Descend west and then climb northwest to the 9,388-foot summit.

Sitgreaves Mountain has a broad grassy top which offers magnificent views. In particular, you get a fine picture of the west side of San Francisco Mountain.

For the return, you can hike almost directly south to get to your parking place, but get well-oriented before you start. First, descend south down the grassy slope of Sitgreaves Mountain. As you enter the forest, follow the major drainage that leads back to the starting point, and pick out the easiest route through the forest. Lower down, there is a multitude of vehicle tracks that lead up into the area north of road 75. If you come out to road 75 west of the starting point, as we did, turn left and follow the road back to your vehicle. It is very important to notice the landmarks on the roads as you drive in on road 75 and road 794 so you can recognize your position if you come out west of the starting point.

■

4

Kendrick Peak

Kendrick Peak.

General description: A fine hike on excellent trail
Hiking distance: 6 miles
Starting elevation: 7,980 feet
High point: 10,418 feet
Elevation gain: 2,500 feet
Maps: 7.5 minute Kendrick Peak;
  Kaibab National Forest

．

K endrick Peak is an isolated summit northwest of San Francisco Mountain with a lookout tower on top. Unlike many peaks with lookouts, Kendrick Peak and its flanks are roadless. A fine trail from a well-constructed trailhead area leads to the summit. The area around Kendrick Peak is in the Kendrick Mountain Wilderness.

From Interstate 40 west of Flagstaff, take exit 185 at Bellemont. Drive west along the north service road to forest road 171. Turn right and follow road 171 north eleven miles to a junction with road 171A. Turn right and drive north one mile to the end of the road at a trailhead parking area.

There is no difficulty in following the well-graded trail from the trailhead to the 10,418-foot summit. The trail winds east and then makes a sharp turn left west to the top. Kendrick Peak with its lookout tower and isolated position makes an attractive viewpoint.

■

5

Hochderffer Hills and White Horse Hills

Humphreys Peak and Agassiz Peak from Hochderffer Hills.

General description: Pleasant hikes on vehicle tracks and
  through woods
Hiking distances: 7 miles and 2 miles
Starting elevation: 7,968 and 8,500 feet
High points: 9,170 and 9,065 feet
Elevation gains: 1,300 and 600 feet
Maps: 7.5 minute Kendrick Peak;
  7.5 minute Wing Mountain;
  7.5 minute White Horse Hills;
  Coconino National Forest

.

These hills north of Flagstaff are broad-based with gently sloping sides. The hikes are easy off-trail walks in wooded areas, but the summits offer little views.

Hochderffer Hills are circled by roads, but these roads are of doubtful quality and may be impassable when wet. Therefore, the hike described starts at the highway. If road conditions permit you to drive closer, you can shorten the hike accordingly.

Drive north from Flagstaff on US 180. Eleven and a half miles beyond the turnoff to the Snow Bowl, find what may be an unmarked dirt road leading to the right. This point is indicated by an elevation of 7968 on the topographic map. Park near the highway west of a fence line.

Hike east on the dirt road and turn right at a junction after one-tenth of a mile. Here you are on forest road 151E. Stay on this road as it climbs south and southeast. If you are walking, you can judge whether you would have preferred to drive. If you are driving, you can judge whether you would have preferred to walk.

Two and one-quarter miles bring you to a cylindrical, green water tank on the left side of the road. There is a fenced catchment facility just up the hillside from the water tank.

At the tank, leave the road, turn left, and hike up the slope northeast. Stay left of a fence line as the route first goes through thick timber and then through scattered trees. Go over a false summit and climb through an area of huge trees. The fence turns left, so you must cross it to walk the short, remaining distance to the summit.

The high point at 9,170 feet is under a large dead tree standing amidst enough other trees to obstruct any distant view. Find your way back to the fence which will help guide you back down the correct ridge to the water tank.

If you want an outstanding view from one of the Hochderffer Hills, you can climb a ridge point southwest of the green water tank. Hike south up the road a quarter mile beyond the water tank. Then hike west up a steep vehicle track that climbs two hundred feet in a surprisingly short distance. The views from this barren ridge point are unobscured. Humphreys Peak and Agassiz Peak are particularly magnificent here.

White Horse Hills are a little more than three miles east of Hochderffer Hills. The walk to the high point of White Horse Hills is shorter and easier, but just as much route finding may be needed.

Drive on US 180 a half mile north of the parking place for the hike to Hochderffer Hills, a total of twelve miles north of the turnoff to the Snow Bowl. Turn right on forest road 151 and drive almost two miles to road 418. Turn left and drive two miles east on road 418. Here you are south of White Horse Hills in a pass at 8,500 feet between White Horse Hills and San Francisco Mountain. Park here.

The topographic map is helpful in navigating the mile of distance and 565 feet of net elevation gain to the high point of White Horse Hills. There are a number of vehicle tracks that make the walking easier. Head generally north slightly to the right of the high point, between the highest hill and some slightly lower hills to the east. Bear left toward higher ground to finally reach the 9,065-foot summit, which doesn't offer much of a view.

■

6

Agassiz Peak
and Humphreys Peak

Frost-covered ridge from Agassiz Peak to Humphreys Peak.

General description: A fine hike mostly on trail to the two
    highest summits in Arizona
Hiking distance: 9 miles
Starting elevation: 9,600 feet
High point: 12,356 and 12,633 feet
Elevation gain: 3,800 feet
Maps: 7.5 minute Humphreys Peak;
    Coconino National Forest

Agassiz Peak
from the ridge
to Humphreys
Peak.

Humphreys Peak at 12,633 feet is the highest summit in Arizona. Agassiz Peak, less than three hundred feet lower, is separated from Humphreys by an 11,780-foot saddle and one and a half miles. These two summits, the only mountains in the state above twelve thousand feet, can both be climbed in what for many would be a long day hike. Others may prefer to climb these two summits on separate hikes. Humphreys Peak can be climbed by an all-trail hike. Agassiz Peak may be climbed along the service road to the ski lift plus a well-beaten path from the top of the lift to the summit. A loop trip to climb both peaks is described here.

Drive west from Flagstaff on US 180 several miles to the well-marked road to the Snow Bowl. Turn north and drive to the ski area, finding a parking place in the upper parking lot.

Hike east up the service road under the ski lift. This takes you from a starting elevation of 9,600 feet to 11,600 feet at timberline on the west side of Agassiz Peak. It is possible to shorten the hike by riding the ski lift if it is operating.

From the top of the ski lift, hike east to the summit

of Agassiz Peak, following a well-beaten path through the rocks. The final climb of 750 vertical feet brings you to the 12,356-foot summit, an outstanding viewpoint well above the timber. Humphreys Peak stands out to the north, making the next goal readily apparent.

Hike north along the ridge toward Humphreys Peak, descending to the 11,780-foot saddle before the final climb to the summit. Walking is fairly easy on the broad open ridge, with beaten paths to follow. Finally at Humphreys Peak you are at 12,633 feet, the high point of the state. The open rocky summit offers unsurpassed vistas, only limited by the quality of the air.

Return toward the saddle between Humphreys Peak and Agassiz Peak. Near the saddle you can pick up a trail that leads back to the Snow Bowl. The trail winds through the forest as it gets lower and eventually brings you back to the parking area at the base of the ski lift.

■

7

Doyle Peak
and Fremont Peak

Doyle Peak and Fremont Peak from Rees Peak.

■

General description: A long strenuous climb on trails and
   rugged ridges
Hiking distance: 14 miles
Starting elevation: 8,024 feet
High points: 11,460 and 11,969 feet
Elevation gain: 4,700 feet
Maps: 7.5 minute Humphreys Peak;
   Coconino National Forest

.

F remont Peak and Doyle Peak are summits on a ridge that extends east from Agassiz Peak. Fremont and Doyle are the third and fourth highest summits in Arizona. The two peaks are best approached from the south via the saddle between the two peaks, a saddle whose name is questionable.

The topographic map shows Fremont Saddle to be between Doyle Peak and Fremont Peak, and Doyle Saddle to be between Fremont Peak and Agassiz Peak. It would seem more logical for the saddle names to be reversed. In any event, the route goes to the saddle that is between Doyle Peak and Fremont Peak.

The hike starts near Schultz Pass, a crossing south of San Francisco Mountain and north of Elden Mountain. Forest road 420 crosses Schultz Pass on its way from US 180 in the northwestern part of Flagstaff to US 89 northeast of the city. The approach from US 180 requires the least driving off of a main highway. From US 180 in the northwestern part of Flagstaff, turn north on the Schultz Pass Road and drive five and a half winding miles to Schultz Pass.

Find a jeep road, forest road 522, leaving the Schultz Pass Road on the north side. This junction is opposite a pond known as Schultz Tank that is south of the Schultz Pass Road. Park passenger cars here.

Hike north up the winding jeep road as it makes several switchbacks and finally becomes a trail at the wilderness boundary. Follow the trail as it climbs to the saddle at 10,780 feet between Doyle Peak and Fremont Peak.

Turn right at the saddle and climb seven-hundred vertical feet to the 11,460-foot summit of Doyle Peak. It may be easier to bear off to the right to find a more gradual route through the rocks and scattered brush. The long flat summit area has its high point at the extreme northeastern end.

Return to the saddle and climb west up the steep brushy ridge to Fremont Peak. This tedious rocky climb of twelve-hundred vertical feet brings you to the 11,969-foot high point that offers a variety of fine vistas.

The ridge to the west descends through another saddle and extends up to Agassiz Peak. To the north is the Inner Basin with Humphreys Peak on the left and the ridge extending right to Aubineau Peak and Rees Peak.

Return east toward Doyle Peak to the saddle and turn right to descend south down the trail.

■

8

Schultz Peak

Fremont Peak from the summit of Schultz Peak.

General description: A ridge climb through grassy meadows
    to a flat summit
Hiking distance: 5 miles
Starting elevation: 8,120 feet
High point: 10,083 feet
Elevation gain: 2,200 feet
Maps: 7.5 minute Sunset Crater West;
    7.5 minute Humphreys Peak;
    Coconino National Forest

S chultz Peak is not a true summit, as it is only a named point on the ridge south of Doyle Peak. The high point is hard to locate among the scattered trees, although there is a grassy meadow just below the summit. The ridge leading to Schultz Peak from the south offers a fine approach through sparse timber.

Drive to Schultz Pass as in the hike to Doyle Peak and Fremont Peak, hike #7. Drive less than a quarter mile east of Schultz tank on forest road 420 to a junction with road 146 that leads northeast. Drive northeast on road 146 barely more than a half mile to an old vehicle track leading north. Park north of road 146 at the barrier that now closes this old road to vehicles.

Hike up the old vehicle track to its end and then bear right on game trails to gain the crest of the ridge. Turn left and climb up the ridge through grassy meadows and patches of timber. After a climb of 1,700 vertical feet from the starting point, you reach a false summit at 9,822 feet in a small meadow. The route continues north, descending slightly along a narrow ridge. It then climbs to a vast flat meadow. Bear left across the meadow and descend slightly through a sparsely wooded area. Climb gradually northwest through another large meadow to the 10,083-foot high point.

Some trees near the high point make the exact summit difficult to locate. The trees also obscure the view from the summit, although excellent views can be obtained from the meadows along the ascent ridge and from points near the summit.

Return the way you came unless you want to be adventuresome, possess the topographic maps, and have a good sense of direction. In that case, you can descend the ridge directly south from the Schultz Peak summit, bear left at the bottom, and find your way back to the starting point.

■

9

Sugarloaf

.

General description: A short steep climb up a timbered slope
Hiking distance: 2 miles
Starting elevation: 8,540 feet
High point: 9,283 feet
Elevation gain: 750 feet
Maps: 7.5 minute Sunset Crater West;
Coconino National Forest

.

S ugarloaf is a flat, wooded summit east of the high
peaks of San Francisco Mountain. Its short ascent is
a steep hike through open timber.

From Flagstaff, drive north on US 89 to forest road
552. Road 552 leaves the highway on the west side
three-quarters of a mile north of the side road that
leads east to Sunset Crater National Monument. Drive
west on road 552, passing left of huge cinder piles.
Just over a mile from the highway, turn right at a
junction. Bypass a gravel pit and drive northwest as
the narrow but good gravel road climbs around the
scenic north side of Sugarloaf. Continue around the
mountain to the south until you reach a broad, marshy
meadow, known as Lockett Meadow, on the right. Find
a good place to park near a small pond.
Hike southeast and east along a primitive road and
an abandoned road to a saddle south of Sugarloaf. Turn

left and climb more steeply to the north through open timber. After ascending five hundred vertical feet, the terrain suddenly flattens out. Continue north a couple of hundred yards through the trees to the 9,283-foot high point.

■

10

Rees Peak
and Aubineau Peak

■

General description: A strenuous hike with some steep rock
scrambling and an optional scree-slope descent
Hiking distance: 10 miles
Starting elevation: 8,540 feet
High points: 11,474 and 11,838 feet
Elevation gain: 3,600 feet
Maps: 7.5 minute Sunset Crater West;
7.5 minute Humphreys Peak;
Coconino National Forest

■

R ees Peak and Aubineau Peak are two named points
on the ridge running northeast and east from
Humphreys Peak. The ascent gives a taste of alpine
climbing with a rocky ridge climb and a descent that
can be made on a scree slope. The climb is rougher
than the figures in the heading would indicate,
although the return can be easier if you enjoy scree-
slope descents.

Drive to Lockett Meadow as in the hike to Sugarloaf,
hike #9. The trailhead is on the southwestern side of
the meadow. It may be better to park on the northeastern side of Lockett Meadow, near the small pond,
unless the roads to the trailhead are dry and in good
condition.
Hike or drive on the dirt roads to the southwestern

side of Lockett Meadow. The route starts west on a service road to the Inner Basin, closed to vehicles by a locked gate. Hike up the road almost two miles to a junction at some water facility buildings. Turn right at the junction and walk along a level fire road that leads toward Bear Jaw Canyon and Aubineau Canyon. This road circles the east side of Rees Peak, and by walking a mile you get to the side of the peak where the climbing is more gradual.

Leave the road on the left, in an area of scattered aspen trees, and climb west. The grade is steady for the tiring climb of some two-thousand vertical feet to the 11,474-foot summit of Rees Peak. The first portion is through fairly open timber and the footing becomes more rocky as you get closer to the summit. The terrain finally levels out. Some rock hopping on the ill-defined ridge brings you to the high point on the west end of the almost-flat summit area.

Since Rees Peak is not a true summit, there is only a two-hundred-foot descent to the saddle between Rees Peak and Aubineau Peak. The descent west to the saddle is steep and rocky and you should look for easy ways around some rock outcrops. Continue west across the broad saddle. Stay left of the crest of the ridge as you climb to the rocky 11,838-foot summit of Aubineau Peak. The climb is six-hundred vertical feet through scattered vegetation on gravel slopes and over large rocks.

The views from both Rees Peak and Aubineau Peak are superlative. You can see the Inner Basin surrounded by Humphreys Peak, Agassiz Peak, Fremont Peak, and Doyle Peak from right to left. Flat lands and many lower summits can be seen to the north and east.

Return to the saddle between Aubineau Peak and Rees Peak. From the saddle you can retrace your steps over Rees Peak to the starting point, or you can follow an alternate route if you like a steep scree-slope descent.

If you choose the steeper descent, turn right at the saddle and head south down the steep slope toward the Inner Basin. Follow the patches of scree as you make your swift sliding descent on a route that would be a poor choice for the climb. Lower down, bear to the left and pick out the easiest route as the grade becomes much more gradual. If you follow along a gully leading southeast, you will eventually meet a road near the junction at the water facility buildings. From the junction, return on the road that leads down to Lockett Meadow.

■

11

Elden Mountain
and Little Elden Mountain

·

General description: A drive to a summit and a short hike
   along a wooded ridge
Hiking distance: 2 miles
Starting elevation: 8,500 feet
High points: 9,018 feet; drive to 9,299 feet
Elevation gain: 700 feet
Maps: 7.5 minute Sunset Crater West;
   7.5 minute Flagstaff East;
   Coconino National Forest

·

E lden Mountain is just north of Flagstaff. Its
   9,299-foot summit provides a fine view of the city
from more than three thousand feet above. A road
leads to the top of Elden Mountain. Little Elden
Mountain is a 9,018-foot named ridge point northeast
of Elden Mountain. Schultz Pass separates Elden
Mountain and Little Elden Mountain from San Francisco
Mountain to the north. Little Elden Mountain can be
climbed with a short off-trail walk through the timber
from the road to Elden Mountain.

From US 180 in the northwestern part of Flagstaff,
drive north on the Schultz Pass Road. After a half mile,
where the Schultz Pass Road turns sharply from east to
north, continue east on a road that becomes forest road
557. Follow this road all the way to the top of Elden

Mountain. Aside from the many communications facilities that clutter the top, the summit of Elden Mountain offers fantastic views of the area. Flagstaff can be seen below to the south and southwest. San Francisco Mountain stands out to the north. Sunset Crater is to the northeast.

For the hike to Little Elden Mountain, drive two miles back down Elden Mountain to a point where the road turns sharply left from northeast to northwest. Park here at an elevation of 8,500 feet.

Hike east up the slope through the timber to the crest of the ridge at 8,820 feet. Turn left and follow the ridge north. Hike over a high point of 8,940 feet and descend eighty feet to a saddle. Continue to follow the ridge as it bends northeast. Climb gradually to the 9,018-foot summit. The exact high point is not easy to find in the timber and there is little view from the summit.

■

12

Two Summits on the Kaibab Plateau

·

General description: Short walks to flat high points
Hiking distances: Three hikes of less than a mile each
Starting elevation: 9,160 feet
High point: 9,240 feet
Elevation gain: 100 feet
Maps: 15 minute De Motte Park (essential);
   Kaibab National Forest (essential)

·

T he Kaibab Plateau is a vast high area north of the
   Grand Canyon. The highest portions rise above
nine thousand feet. The plateau is so flat that it is
difficult to tell where the high points are, and there are
no real mountain summits.

The 15 minute De Motte Park topographic map
shows six closed contours of 9,200 feet, but none
higher. So the high points of the Kaibab Plateau
interpolate to 9,240 feet.

Two of these 9,200-foot contours are close to one
another a mile and a half southwest of Kaibab Lodge.
The lodge is on Arizona 67 which leads to the North
Rim of the Grand Canyon. A side road west of Arizona
67 passes over the larger contour and close to the
smaller contour. A short walk should get you to the
high point of each of these contours. One of these
high points is one of the "summits" on the Kaibab
Plateau.

A separate high area is east of Arizona 67, the road to the North Rim. The high points east of the highway are separated from those southwest of Kaibab Lodge by an 8,827-foot saddle at the North Rim Entrance Station, so technically there are two "peaks" of 9,240 feet on the Kaibab Plateau, one west of the highway and the other east of it.

One portion of the high area east of Arizona 67 consists of three closed contours near forest road 219 to Marble Viewpoint. These three high points are northwest of South Canyon Spring.

Then there is another 9,200-foot contour in section 17 near forest road 610 that runs along the Grand Canyon National Park boundary on its way toward Saddle Mountain. There is no way to tell if this point is higher than the highest of the points northwest of South Canyon Spring. In summary, there are four 9,200-foot contours east of Arizona 67, the three near the road to Marble Viewpoint and the one near forest road 610. It would be necessary to hike to each of these high points to be sure of reaching the "summit" east of Arizona 67.

The Kaibab Plateau has not yet been mapped with the larger scale 7.5-minute quadrangles, so more detailed mapping may reveal other high points. Only the most dedicated "peak baggers" would be interested in searching out such "summits," anyway.

Frank', we didn't think hiking to these high points was worth a special trip to the Kaibab Plateau, so we haven't been to them yet. We plan to try to find them on our next trip to the North Rim. There are many more interesting things to do at the Grand Canyon, so we will only look for these summits as a means of stretching our legs on the long drive to the North Rim.

■

Central Ranges

N one of the summits in central Arizona reach nine thousand feet, but there are seven ranges whose high points exceed seven thousand feet. These ranges are in the Prescott National Forest and the Tonto National Forest.

The highest peaks of the Bradshaw, Sierra Ancha and Pinal Mountains can be reached by automobile. The Juniper Mountains and the Santa Maria Mountains, in the northern part of the Prescott National Forest, have fine trails to their high points. The climb to the summit of Granite Mountain near Prescott is challenging. Mazatzal Peak, the high point of the Mazatzal Mountains, is the most difficult summit to climb of the high points of mountain ranges in this central area.

13

Juniper Mesa

On the rocky south edge of Juniper Mesa.

General description: A pleasant hike on a trail
up a canyon
Hiking distance: 6 miles
Starting elevation: 6,340 feet
High point: 7,100 feet
Elevation gain: 1,000 feet
Maps: 7.5 minute Juniper Mountains;
Prescott National Forest

.

J uniper Mesa is the high point of the Juniper
   Mountains. The mesa is so flat that it is difficult to
find the location of the high point, so we must rely on
the topographic map. The map indicates that the high
point, at an interpolated elevation of 7,100 feet, is near
a fine trail that leads across the mesa.

The starting point for the hike is quite remote, and
to get there requires many miles of driving on back
roads, but the trip is well worth it. The access road is
off of forest road 6 that runs between Prescott and
Interstate 40. From the north, leave Interstate 40 on exit
123 at Seligman. Drive south on a road toward Walnut
Creek that becomes forest road 6 after it enters Prescott
National Forest. Twenty-five miles from the interstate,
turn west onto forest road 7. This intersection can be
reached from the south by driving forty-three miles
from Prescott, leaving the west part of town on the
Williamson Valley Road.
   Drive west and southwest on forest road 7 for seven
and a half miles to the end of the road, which is a
quarter of a mile beyond Pine Springs. This trip may
require a high-clearance vehicle if the road is wet or if
it hasn't been graded recently. Park at the end of the
road, which is at the wilderness boundary.
   Hike southwest on the old roadbed, now closed to
vehicles, as you enter the Juniper Basin Wilderness.
This roadbed climbs gradually along Pine Creek for a
mile and a half. The roadbed narrows into a trail,
steepens, and climbs to the top of the mesa. The trail
stays right of a fence line. Once on the mesa, you
reach a trail junction near a gate at an elevation of
7,060 feet.
   At the trail junction, the terrain on the mesa is

practically level. The rocky soil supports a variety of plant life, including the alligator juniper which gives the mesa its name. Make a sharp left turn, almost a hairpin, passing through the gate at the trail junction. Look for blazes on the trees to mark the beginning of the Juniper Springs Trail, which leads toward the high point. Follow this excellent well-marked trail as it descends one hundred vertical feet. Hike southeast across a minor saddle and begin a climb up a narrow ridge, as the trail is marked by large cairns. Continue almost a half mile from the minor saddle to reach the high point on the trail. Slightly higher ground to the right of the trail is the location we judged to be the 7,100-foot summit of the mesa, and consequently, the high point of the Juniper Mountains.

While there are no good views from the high point, you can get excellent views from the precipitous, south edge of the mesa. Several good view points are just a few yards south of the trail.

According to the topographic map, the trail leads on east across the mesa, passing several points that are almost as high as the indicated summit before descending to Juniper Spring.

■

14

Hyde Creek Mountain

Building on the summit of Hyde Creek Mountain.

General description: A fine trail hike
Hiking distance: 6 miles
Starting elevation: 5,820 feet
High point: 7,270 feet
Elevation gain: 1,500 feet
Maps: 7.5 minute Camp Wood;
    Prescott National Forest

．

H yde Creek Mountain is the high point of the Santa Maria Mountains, a range northwest of Prescott. An excellent trail leads to the top and there is a lookout building on the summit. The summit area offers superb views and the hike makes a delightful outing in remote country.

   Drive north from the northwestern part of Prescott on the Williamson Valley Road. Take this paved road, which becomes forest road 6, north for twenty-two miles to the intersection with forest road 21 on the left. This intersection can be reached from the north by a continuation of the long drive on forest road 6 used for the hike to Juniper Mesa, hike #13. Turn west from forest road 6 onto forest road 21 and drive about fifteen miles to Camp Wood. Just north of road 21 at Camp Wood, pick up road 95C and drive two miles northwest to the trailhead.
   Hike northwest up the good trail as it leaves from the area of a corral, climbs somewhat, levels out across a broad meadow, and then climbs up a valley. The trail then climbs out onto the southeast ridge of Hyde Creek Mountain and circles the south side of the mountain to gain the southwest ridge. It then turns back to the east for the final climb to the summit. The red lookout building is in view during parts of the climb.
   Southwest of 7,270-foot Hyde Creek Mountain is Camp Wood Mountain which is only a few feet lower at an interpolated elevation of 7,260 feet. By circling around the lookout building on Hyde Creek Mountain, you can gain unobstructed views in any direction. Juniper Mesa stands out to the north. The Apache Creek Wilderness is in the area north of Hyde Creek

Mountain.

There are other trails on the flanks of Hyde Creek Mountain, so carefully work your way back on the same trail to the starting point.

Hyde Creek Mountain is shown as "Hyde Mountain" on some maps, but a U.S. Board on Geographic Names decision in late 1986 established the name Hyde Creek Mountain.

■

15

Granite Mountain

Granite Mountain.

General description: A hike on trail and some rock scrambling along a cairned off-trail route
Hiking distance: 9 miles
Starting elevation: 5,580 feet
High point: 7,626 feet
Elevation gain: 2,400 feet
Maps: 7.5 minute Iron Springs; 7.5 minute Jerome Canyon; Prescott National Forest

.

M ajestic Granite Mountain rises as an unmistakable
landmark west of Prescott. Its unique combination
of cliffs and large rocks mixed with varied vegetation
make this trip a truly memorable outing. While some
might argue that Granite Mountain is not a true
mountain range, its extent and the subsidiary summits
around its flanks make it qualify for the mountain-range
category. On the other hand, no one would argue that
such a fine hike should not be included here. Those
who may not feel qualified for the route-finding climb
to the summit can enjoy the trail portion of this hike.

Drive three miles west from Prescott on the Iron
Springs Road. Turn right and drive five miles northwest
on forest road 374 to a trailhead parking area at the
road's end.

Hike a mile and a half northwest on the gradually
climbing trail to Blair Pass at 5,940 feet. At the pass,
turn right at a trail junction. Climb north on switchbacks as you savor the beauties of the Granite Mountain
Wilderness. The trail turns sharply right to take you
southeast along the south side of a ridge. The trail
then reaches a flat area and bends south. In this area
you can view the top of Granite Mountain off to the
east.

Those who want an all-trail hike can continue on the
trail another half mile to a view point on the south
side of the mountain. Those who want to climb the
peak should leave the trail on the left and head east. It
would be possible to find your way to the summit
without benefit of a marked route, but there probably
would be considerable trial and error in working your
way around the large boulders. Thus it is best to follow
the cairns that lead east from the trail.

The cairned route to the summit is an interesting one to follow as it winds its way through the brush and around the large boulders. Sometimes it takes time to spot the next cairn. Some rock scrambling is required here and there. The climb goes generally east, then northeast, and then north. The marked route climbs to the high point from the east side of the peak.

The 7,626-foot summit consists of large rock slabs that make a nice lunch spot. The views are grandiose in all directions. The Santa Maria Mountains are north and the Bradshaw Mountains are to the south. Southeast you can look down to the city of Prescott. Carefully follow the cairned route back to the trail for the return.

■

16

Mount Union

•

General description: A long drive to the summit with a
   variety of possible routes
Hiking distance: Optional
High point: 7,979 feet
Maps: 7.5 minute Groom Creek;
   Prescott National Forest (essential)

•

T he Bradshaw Mountains are south of Prescott in
   the Prescott National Forest. Mount Union at 7,979
feet is the high point. These wooded mountains are
interlaced with enough roads to satisfy the exploratory
needs of the most venturesome backroad driver. The
Bradshaw Mountains were named for William D.
Bradshaw, an early settler in the area. They were once
called the Silver Range.

   There are so many ways to drive to Mount Union
that we wouldn't want to suggest a best one. You can
appreciate this when you look at the road system in
the Bradshaw Mountains on the Prescott National
Forest map, which we think is essential for this drive.
   You can approach Mount Union from Mayer or
Poland Junction on Arizona 69, from either of two
roads out of Prescott, from Interstate 17 or from US 89.
Our suggestion is to look at the Prescott National
Forest map and choose your route. The final approach

to the summit is from the west.

There is a lookout tower at the summit of Mount Union. There are hiking trails in the Bradshaw Mountains, but there doesn't appear to be any way to hike up Mount Union and avoid the roads.

■

17

Mazatzal Peak

On the Barnhardt Trail toward Mazatzal Peak.

General description: A long hike partly on trail with some rugged bushwhacking and rock scrambling
Hiking distance: 17 miles
Starting elevation: 4,200 feet
High point: 7,903 feet
Elevation gain: 4,200 feet
Maps: 7.5 minute Mazatzal Peak (essential);
Tonto National Forest

.

M azatzal Peak at 7,903 feet is the high point of the Mazatzal Mountains. It is the only Arizona summit that is the high point of two counties, sitting on the border of Gila and Yavapai counties in central Arizona. There is no easy route to the summit, but the ascent makes a satisfying climb in a beautiful wilderness area. Fine trails in the Mazatzal Wilderness surround Mazatzal Peak, but the routes to the summit after you leave the trail require bushwhacking, rock scrambling, and route finding.

Take Arizona 87 to a point some three miles north of the junction with Arizona 188 and twelve miles south of Payson. Turn west on forest road 419 and drive five miles to the end of the road at a trailhead parking area.

Our suggested ascent route follows the Barnhardt Trail six miles west to the range crest. The route then follows the range crest south to the summit.

Hike west on the Barnhardt Trail from the trailhead parking area, bearing right as the Shake Tree Trail goes southwest to the left. You soon enter the Mazatzal Wilderness. After four miles, at 5,940 feet, take the left fork as the right fork trail leads to Sandy Saddle. Two more miles brings you to the range crest at 6,020 feet.

There was said to be an old fire road leading south up the range crest, but recent efforts by a number of hikers to locate it have failed. Unless you can find such a road, a suggested route is to follow the trail west a few yards beyond the range crest, find the most open area, and turn left to bushwhack southeast up the ridge.

Climb to a flat area at 6,460 feet and continue up the ridge as it becomes narrower and more rocky. Some rock scrambling and avoiding of obstacles is needed in

On the summit
of Mazatzal
Peak.

a long section of the narrow ridge. Finally, at 7,180
feet, the ridge broadens and the hiking is easier in the
open forest. Bear left around a false summit 7,823 feet
high and head across a rocky flat area to make the
final ascent to the high point. The rocky top of
Mazatzal Peak offers fine views in all directions.

To make a loop trip, a descent down Suicide Ridge
can be made. This ridge runs northeast, to the right
(east) of the ridge you ascended. Return to the flat
rocky area north of the summit and head northeast on
the crest of the ridge. The ridge is delightfully open for
the first mile and a half, as you climb over ridge points
of 7,592 and 7,500 feet.

At 7,403 feet, stay left on the spur ridge north as
Suicide Ridge curls east. Just as you wonder why you
didn't come up this way, the ridge gradually becomes
more brushy, and bushwhacking and careful route
finding are required. After descending to the 6,000-foot
level, bear right and come off the ridge crest into a
drainage east of the ridge. Follow this drainage north
to meet the Barnhardt Trail at 5,540 feet. Turn right and
follow the trail back to the trailhead.

Ascents of Mazatzal Peak have been made from the
south and the east from the Shake Tree Trail. Other

routes are up the main north drainage, which the Barnhardt Trail crosses at 5,920 feet, and south through the forest west of this drainage.

For those desiring a more leisurely backpacking approach, good camping areas can be found along the Barnhardt Trail. In any event, by whatever route you may use, an ascent of Mazatzal Peak is an authentic and gratifying wilderness experience.

■

18

Aztec Peak

Along the road to Aztec Peak.

General description: A scenic drive to a high summit,
  with an optional short hike to an adjoining ridge point
Hiking distance: Optional or 2 miles
High point: 7,748 feet
Maps: 7.5 minute Aztec Peak;
  Tonto National Forest

Workman Creek
Falls near the
road to
Aztec Peak.

Y ou can drive to Aztec Peak, the high point of the
Sierra Ancha Mountains in central Arizona.
Nevertheless, there is good hiking in the Sierra Anch
Mountains, particularly in the Sierra Ancha Wilderness
portion of the Tonto National Forest.

The road to Aztec Peak is from Arizona 288 some
twenty miles north of where it leaves Arizona 88 north
of Globe. Turn east on forest road 487 and follow it
seven miles, all the way to the summit. Portions of the
road can get muddy, so it is best to avoid this trip in
wet weather. There is a large lookout tower on Aztec
Peak that can give you even better views than you get
from the summit area.

When we visited Aztec Peak, neither the map nor
our judgment made it certain that Aztec was higher
than a ridge point a mile north. So we hiked over to
that ridge point just to be sure we were getting to the
high point of the Sierra Ancha Mountains. Now the
new topographic map shows that the ridge point to the

Author near the summit of Aztec Peak.

north is 7,732 feet high, just sixteen feet lower than Aztec Peak. Nevertheless, the hike over to the northern ridge point, which is labeled "Murphy" on the new topographic map, was so interesting that we would recommend it.

To hike to Murphy, descend directly north from Aztec Peak through the scattered trees. You will pass near a switchback in the ascent road on your right and descend into a 7,540-foot saddle. Continuing north, the route passes over a minor false summit and climbs gradually to Murphy. There are some rock outcrops to skirt or climb over on the way. Startling views can be gained from the cliff edges on the east side of the route. The hike is a little over two miles round trip with only a few hundred feet of elevation gain.

During the winter, the road to Aztec Peak is closed by a locked gate near Workman Creek Falls. A walk up the road from the gate is a round trip hike of six miles with an elevation gain of 1,200 feet.

■

19

Pinal Peak

.

General description: A drive to the summit
Hiking distance: Optional
High point: 7,848 feet
Maps: 7.5 minute Pinal Peak;
  Tonto National Forest

.

P inal Peak, the high point of the Pinal Mountains, is
a mountaintop in the Tonto National Forest that can
be visited by a pleasant drive. Near the top, you
emerge from the trees into a flat area that, while
marred by communication facilities, offers enchanting
views of the surrounding mountains and valleys.

The starting point for the drive is at Globe. From just
southeast of the railroad bridge on US 60 and 70 in
Globe, drive south toward the Pinal Mountain
Recreation Area. Follow forest road 112, road 55, and
then road 651 on the winding drive south to the
7,848-foot summit.

The last few miles are steep and may be too rough
for some passenger cars if the road hasn't been graded
recently. Near the top, you pass a summer home area
and then go by a short spur road to Signal Peak.
Signal Peak, a 7,812-foot ridge point, is covered with
communication facilities. A half mile farther, you get to
the Pinal Mountain Recreation Area. It is another half

mile to the top of Pinal Peak.

By maneuvering around the communication towers, you can get excellent views, particularly to the south. The maps show several trails in the Pinal Mountains that would offer long hiking routes to Pinal Peak. They all intersect the road at points below the summit.

■

White Mountains

.

T he White Mountains are in the east central part
of Arizona. They cover a vast area of generally
high terrain. The eastern part of the White Mountains
that borders New Mexico is in the Apache National
Forest. More than half of the nine-thousand-foot
summits of Arizona are in the White Mountains. The
high point is Mount Baldy, at 11,420 feet, on the
border between the Apache National Forest and the
Fort Apache Indian Reservation. Three other summits
in the Apache National Forest exceed ten thousand
feet in elevation.

Many of the White Mountain summits are knolls
with elevations between nine thousand and ten
thousand feet. The general terrain in the area is near
nine thousand feet, so most of the summits require
climbs of only a few hundred vertical feet. The White
Mountains are mostly wooded and there has been
much logging in the forests. As a result, there are
many old and new roads that sometimes are more
confusing than helpful. In some cases, finding a
summit is more challenging than the climb itself.
For the most part, however, the ascents of White
Mountain summits provide pleasant hiking.

The Apache-Sitgreaves National Forests map is a
must to find your way through the maze of back
roads in the White Mountains. The older topographic
maps are helpful, but the roads are not up-to-date.
Part of the adventure of climbing White Mountain
summits is finding the right road to the right
mountain before you start the hike.

■

20

Saint Peters Dome; Whiting Knoll; and Peak 9,387

▪

General description: Three short climbs through meadows
and open forests
Hiking distances: Three hikes of 1 to 2 miles each
Starting elevations: 8,810 to 9,060 feet
High points: 9,348 to 9,636 feet
Elevation gains: 350 to 650 feet per hike
Maps: 7.5 minute Whiting Knoll;
Apache-Sitgreaves National Forests

▪

S aint Peters Dome, Whiting Knoll, and Peak 9,387
are the most northerly of the nine-thousand-foot
peaks in the White Mountains. There should be no
difficulties encountered on the three short climbs.

These three mountains are near forest road 117 that
runs between US 60 and Arizona 260 west of Springerville. To reach forest road 117 from Arizona 260, drive
west from Springerville or east from McNary to about
the midpoint between these towns, where forest road
117 leads north toward Greens Peak. Forest road 117
leaves the highway a mile and a half east of the Fort
Apache Indian Reservation boundary. Follow road 117
as it winds north and circles east of Greens Peak.
South of Greens Peak, there is a junction with forest
road 61 that turns left. Drive almost three miles on
road 117 beyond this junction to a point where the

main road bears left and a side road leads right. This junction is in a meadow at an elevation of 8,997 feet. Start the hike to Saint Peters Dome from this meadow.

Walk north across the meadow and then hike up through the gradually steepening forest. There are about four hundred feet of rather steep climbing before the grade slackens near the top. The total climb is 650 feet for the two-mile hike to Saint Peters Dome. The summit is mostly wooded but some partial views can be obtained from near the 9,636-foot summit.

For the hike to Whiting Knoll, drive on forest road 117 five miles past the junction with forest road 61. This point is nearly one-half mile beyond the junction with road 64. The hike starts at the edge of a broad meadow with 9,348-foot Whiting Knoll to the north. Walk north across the meadow and begin a gradual ascent. Continue north as the grade becomes steeper in the open forest. At the top, there is no view, but you can get nice views of Saint Peters Dome and Greens Peak on the way up or down. The two-mile hike to Whiting Knoll has an elevation gain of 650 feet.

To climb Peak 9,387, the shortest of these three hikes, return to the intersection of forest road 117 with road 64. Turn right and drive one-half mile northwest on road 64 to a junction. Turn left and drive two and a half miles southwest on road 583. This puts you southeast of Peak 9,387 at an elevation of 9,060 feet.

Cross a fence northwest of the road and climb northwest. The walk is mostly on grass through scattered large trees. There are some rock outcrops near the top. The summit is flat and offers limited view points. The hike is only a mile with 350 feet of climbing.

■

21

Greens Peak; Grassy Top; Peak 9,947; Peak 9,913; and Peak 9,559

View south from Greens Peak.

General description: A drive to a lookout tower, two hikes through grassy meadows, and two hikes through dense forests

Hiking distances: Four hikes of 1 to 2 miles each

Starting elevations: 9,210 to 9,550 feet

High points: 9,559 to 9,947 feet; drive to 10,133 feet

Elevation gains: 350 to 600 feet per hike

Maps: 7.5 minute Greens Peak;
   Apache-Sitgreaves National Forests

·

A drive to Greens Peak with a climb of four nearby summits makes a varied day's outing. Greens Peak, at 10,133 feet, is the highest summit in the Apache National Forest with a road to the top. It has a lookout tower and is covered with communications equipment. Three of the other four summits are the highest "nine-thousanders" in the Apache National Forest.

From Arizona 260 midway between Springerville and McNary, drive north on forest road 117. When you reach a junction south of Greens Peak, turn left (northwest) on road 61 and soon thereafter continue straight (north) on road 61C when road 61 veers left. Follow this road to the summit. Try to make this drive up the peak during the posted visiting hours in order to visit the lookout tower.

Two of the remaining four peaks can be climbed from the same parking area. Each is a hike of a little over a mile with an elevation gain of four hundred feet. Start from road 117 at a 9,550-foot saddle between the two peaks, almost a quarter of a mile south of the junction of road 117 and road 61.

Peak 9,910, which we have termed "Grassy Top," can be climbed on an all-grass route. Hike southwest from the saddle, staying southeast of the trees. Then bend to the northwest and follow the open ridge to the summit of Grassy Top. There are open views in all directions.

For Peak 9,947, hike east from the same parking place. You can curve north and follow the open grassy ridge almost to the summit. The last short stretch to the summit is in the trees, so the best views are shortly before you reach the summit area.

The last two peaks are approached from two other locations. A good starting point for Peak 9,913 is on forest road 117 roughly two and a half miles north of Arizona 260. Maps show other roads leading somewhat closer to the peak, but such roads are not always passable. Walk west from road 117 across some flat land, aiming for the northeast ridge of the peak. Climb up through the forest using logging tracks where possible to avoid logging debris. Follow the northeast ridge all the way to the summit. There is a strikingly open view to the south from the summit area. The hike is two miles with an elevation gain of six hundred feet.

Peak 9,559 is west of Greens Peak. From the junction of road 61 and road 61C, drive west almost two miles. Park south of the peak at a meadow on the north side of the road. Walk north across this meadow and then climb steeply through the forest. You will reach the south end of a flat summit area and can continue north to the high point. You gain 350 feet of elevation in the mile hike.

■

22

Antelope Mountain; Pole Knoll; and Boardshack Knoll

Looking southwest from Pole Knoll.

General description: Three varied hikes, one up a steep service road, one through a grassy meadow, and one in the forest

Hiking distances: Three hikes of 1 to 3 miles each

Starting elevations: 8,350 to 9,233 feet

High points: 9,003 to 9,793 feet

Elevation gains: 250 to 700 feet per hike

Maps: 7.5 minute Greer;
7.5 minute Greens Peak;
7.5 minute Mount Baldy;
Apache-Sitgreaves National Forests

■

These three mountains are near Arizona 260 west of
Springerville. Antelope Peak is a barren mountain
north of the highway with a plainly visible road
leading to the top. Pole Knoll, across the highway to
the south, has partly grassy and partly forested sides.
Boardshack Knoll is a forested hill north of Mount
Baldy.

Antelope Mountain is on state land (see introduction)
just east and north of the Apache National Forest
boundary. It has a road to the top, but the road is so
steep and rough that most people will prefer to walk.

Drive on Arizona 260 to a point about ten miles west
of Eagar. Turn north on a road that is just east of the
Apache National Forest boundary sign. Drive one-half
mile, passing a corral and going through a gate. Park
on National Forest land shortly beyond the gate, as the
road becomes decidedly worse.

Hike northwest and north along the road as it
gradually ascends and passes between Antelope
Mountain and Ellis Wiltbank Reservoir. The road then
steepens and switches back sharply from a northerly to
a southeasterly direction. The road reaches a flat area
at 8,950 feet with communication facilities ahead to the
east. The summit of Antelope Mountain is to the west,
so make a sharp turn left, leave the road, and hike to
the 9,003-foot high point. The three-mile hike has a
seven-hundred-foot elevation gain. Antelope Mountain
has mostly grassy slopes, with few trees, so the views
are good in all directions.

Pole Knoll is another mountain with good views
from the top. For this hike, drive on Arizona 260 some
five miles farther west from the road to Antelope

Looking south from Boardshack Knoll.

Mountain. Drive south on forest road 113F almost a mile to a road junction. Park near this junction west of Pole Knoll at an elevation of 9,200 feet.

Hike east through the open forest, bearing right of a rocky rib. Then climb through meadows, finally staying right of a fenced-off section near the summit. There is a benchmark on the 9,793-foot high point. The climb is six hundred feet in the three-mile hike. The summit affords magnificent views of the lakes in the valley below, the ski slopes on the hillsides beyond, and Mount Baldy in the distance.

Boardshack Knoll is best approached from a road that runs east of White Mountain Reservoir. From the starting point for the hike to Pole Knoll, drive on south two miles and then take a spur road that continues south as road 113F turns east. This spur road also can be reached from forest road 113 between road 87 and the Fort Apache Indian Reservation. Drive to a point on this spur road that shows as an elevation of 9,233 feet on the topographic map and which is three-quarters of a mile north of road 113. Here you are west of Boardshack Knoll.

Hike east through the open timber and bear left to

the 9,524-foot summit. The entire hike is no more than a mile with three hundred feet of elevation gain. There is no view from the high point, but by moving to the eastern edge of the broad summit area some fine views can be obtained. The views are more pleasing if you can overlook the gravel pit on the southeastern ridge of Boardshack Knoll. No, we didn't find a board shack on the knoll.

■

23

Sizer Knoll; Pool Knoll; Wahl Knoll; Rudd Knoll; and Pat Knoll

Distant view of Greens Peak from Wahl Knoll.

General description: Five walks through grassy meadows
    and timbered slopes
Hiking distances: Five hikes of 1 to 4 miles each
Starting elevations: 9,160 to 9,320 feet
High points: 9,424 to 9,764 feet
Elevation gains: 250 to 450 feet per hike
Maps: 7.5 minute Greer;
    15 minute Big Lake;
    Apache-Sitgreaves National Forests

.

T hese five knolls are north of Big Lake. Four of
them are clearly visible from the vast meadowed
areas north of Big Lake. The fifth, Sizer Knoll, is more
remote and careful navigation is needed to reach its
summit.

Sizer Knoll, a named point but not a true summit,
can be approached by a hike on varied terrain. Several
approaches are possible, but we liked the one from the
south. The entry is off Arizona 273 that runs south
from Arizona 260 three miles west of Eagar. Drive
south on newly-paved Arizona 273 to forest road 409.
Drive west on winding road 409. Within four miles you
can clearly see Sizer Knoll, a wooded summit north up
the valley to the right. This valley looks like a good
approach for the hike to Sizer Knoll, since you have
the objective in view. We started farther along the road,
however, four and a half miles from Arizona 273. Here,
at an elevation of 9,160 feet, a dirt vehicle track heads
west as road 409 turns to the south.

Hike west along the vehicle track and turn right
when another vehicle track is met. Navigate north on
various faint vehicle tracks, finally making a slight
descent to a 9,190-foot saddle and going through a
gate. The climb is then due north to Sizer Knoll, first
through sparse timber and then through larger trees.

The summit of Sizer Knoll, at 9,424 feet, is an area of
large rocks. There is a partial view so that you can look
back and see Hay Lake to the south. Carefully find
your way back to the starting point. The four-mile hike
has an elevation gain of only three hundred feet.

Pool Knoll is west of Arizona 273 some six miles
north of Big Lake. Pool Knoll is only one-half mile east

of forest road 409 and can be approached from that
road. Forest road 409 leads west from Arizona 273
about midway between Arizona 260 and Big Lake. It
winds west and south to meet road 113 west of
Crescent Lake. The starting point for climbing Pool
Knoll is from road 409 west of the knoll at 9,200 feet
near a spur road that circles north of the knoll and
leads to Arizona 273. Don't make the mistake of trying
to drive this spur road as we did to our sorrow. In fact,
road 409 may not be the greatest of roads, either. We
drove north on road 409 from road 113 west of Crescent
Lake, but we haven't tried the northern approach.

Hike east from road 409 toward the high point, first
crossing a broad meadow. You walk over volcanic rocks
as you climb up through the trees. The 9,464-foot
summit of Pool Knoll is rocky, with some trees, and
there is a partial view. We looked for a pool on the
knoll but didn't find one.

There is no problem in finding Wahl Knoll or in
driving to the starting point for the hike. On Arizona
273, a mile south of the intersection with road 409, you
are in the saddle between Wahl Knoll and Rudd Knoll.
This saddle, at 9,320 feet, makes a good starting point
for the two-mile round trip hike to Wahl Knoll.

Hike west through the meadow toward the obvious
high point. There is a fence to cross, after which the
grade becomes a little steeper. The views are outstanding, both on the way up and from the summit. Wahl
Knoll, at 9,764 feet, has trees on its north side but it
gives an open view in other directions.

Rudd Knoll is a named point east of Arizona 273.
It could be climbed from the same parking place that
starts the climb to Wahl Knoll. Rudd Knoll, however, is
wooded on the north and open on the south like Wahl
Knoll, so the best climb is from the south. Walk or

On the
summit of
Rudd Knoll.

drive east a half mile on forest road 90, which goes
south of Rudd Knoll.

Hike north up the grassy slope of Rudd Knoll. Some
rock outcrops are at the 9,560-foot top. The view is
similar to the one from Wahl Knoll, completely open to
the south overlooking the vast meadows in the flat
lands north of Big Lake. The hike of a mile climbs just
250 feet.

Pat Knoll is little more than two miles east of Rudd
Knoll. Pat Knoll is east of forest road 285 that runs
south from Eagar. You may be able to combine a hike
to Pat Knoll with the trip to Rudd Knoll by using forest
road 90 south of Rudd Knoll to get to the starting
point for the hike to Pat Knoll. Otherwise, drive south
from Eagar on forest road 285 twelve miles from
Arizona 260. This puts you a mile south of the junction
with road 60 at 9,320 feet and just west of Pat Knoll.

Hike east from road 285, cross a fence, and walk
through a meadow into an area of scattered trees. Walk

Tower and benchmark cover on the summit of Pat Knoll.

over volcanic rocks in the grass, bearing left to gain the west ridge. Follow the ridge east through open timber to the summit. At the 9,651-foot high point there is a benchmark with a metal cover, a small pipe tower, and a large cairn. There is a good view east from the summit. The two-mile hike climbs 350 feet.

■

24

Mount Baldy

West Fork Little Colorado River near the start of the trail to Mount Baldy.

General description: A fine trail hike to the high point of the
  White Mountains
Hiking distance: 13 miles
Starting elevation: 9,220 feet
High point: 11,420 feet
Elevation gain: 2,400 feet
Maps: 7.5 minute Mount Baldy;
    Apache-Sitgreaves National Forests

.

M any people visit the White Mountains only to climb Mount Baldy, because it is the highest peak in the range. In doing so, they may be missing some fine hiking in other parts of the White Mountains. Nevertheless, the hike to Mount Baldy is one of the premier hiking experiences in Arizona.

Mount Baldy sits astride the boundary between the Apache National Forest and the Fort Apache Indian Reservation. The area surrounding Mount Baldy is in the Mount Baldy Wilderness. There may be a misconception that the summit of Mount Baldy, and thus the high point of the White Mountains, is in the Fort Apache Indian Reservation. This is incorrect, as the high point of Mount Baldy is in the Apache National Forest just east of the Indian reservation boundary.

The confusion on this matter may be because there is a small ridge point, called Baldy Peak, south of Mount Baldy and within the Indian reservation territory. Baldy Peak is labeled on the topographic map with an elevation of 11,403 feet. Mount Baldy to its north is enclosed by a long 11,400-foot contour, but the U.S.G.S. neglected to put an elevation on its high point. The usual procedure in cases of this kind is to interpolate an elevation by adding half the contour interval, in this case twenty feet, making the elevation of Mount Baldy 11,420 feet. The U.S.G.S. in correspondence with us confirmed that no exact elevation was recorded for Mount Baldy and that the best estimate of its elevation is 11,420 feet. If all this is confusing, a close look at the topographic map should make it clear.

Now let's get going toward Mount Baldy. Drive on Arizona 260 between Springerville and McNary to Arizona 273 which leads south just west of the Fort

Along the trail
to Mount Baldy
in mid-October.

Apache Indian Reservation boundary. This road also
becomes forest road 113 after it enters the national
forest. You reach Sheep Crossing a mile and a half
south of the intersection with road 87, at a point where
the road makes a sharp loop to the west. Just north of
a creek crossing at this loop, drive straight west on a
spur road for one-half mile to the road end at a
trailhead parking area.

Hike southwest on the almost level trail as it stays
right of West Fork Little Colorado River. The trail
crosses some meadows, loops around a marshy area,
and finally climbs steeply through the forest on
switchbacks. Following a route not shown on the
topographic map, the trail reaches the northeast ridge
of Mount Baldy and stays near the top or just left of
the ridge crest.

The route breaks out into the open as it approaches
Mount Baldy from the north and then climbs to the
summit. The summit cairn is at the north end of the
long narrow 11,400-foot contour. You can see that the

Looking south toward Baldy Peak from the summit of Mount Baldy.

middle of this narrow ridge, also above 11,400 feet, is considerably lower than the high point. On beyond you see the conical summit of Baldy Peak in the Fort Apache Indian Reservation. Without any background mountains nearly as high, it is easy to see why some may have thought Baldy Peak is higher than the summit of Mount Baldy.

Looking farther in the distance, the views are unexcelled. You can pick out many other major mountain ranges such as the Pinalenos, Galiuros, and Santa Catalinas. The East Fork Trail is another approach to Mount Baldy and is about as long as the trail from Sheep Crossing. It is about four miles by road from the trailhead west of Sheep Crossing to the East Fork trailhead.

■

25

Big Lake Knoll; Peak 9,320; Tank Top; S U Knolls; and Burro Mountain

Lookout tower on Big Lake Knoll.

General description: A drive to a lookout tower and
    four hikes through the forest, partly on old logging roads
Hiking distances: Four hikes of 1 to 3 miles each
Starting elevations: 8,862 to 9,366 feet
High points: 9,320 to 9,880 feet; drive to 9,419 feet
Elevation gains: 300 to 600 feet per hike
Maps: 15 minute Big Lake;
    Apache-Sitgreaves National Forests

.

T hese five mountains surround Big Lake. Big Lake Knoll has a road to the summit and a lookout tower on top. The other summits provide pleasant walks through the forest, but offer little or no views from their tops.

Big Lake Knoll is southeast of Big Lake. Big Lake is some twenty miles south-southwest of Springerville and fifteen miles west of Alpine. There are several ways to get to the Big Lake area. Arizona 273 goes south to Big Lake from three miles west of Eagar on Arizona 260. Arizona 273 also leads to Big Lake from Arizona 260 near the eastern edge of the Fort Apache Indian Reservation. Arizona 273 becomes forest road 113 east of the reservation. Forest road 249 leads to Big Lake from near Alpine. It joins road 113 near Big Lake.

To get to Big Lake Knoll, drive road 249 southeast of Big Lake and take road 249D south. Road 249D curves west and then northwest as it climbs to 9,415 feet at the top of Big Lake Knoll. The lookout tower on Big Lake Knoll gives a good view of the area.

There are two summits on opposite sides of Big Lake that happen to be the same height, 9,320 feet. For Peak 9,320 east of Big Lake, drive east on road 249 a mile and a half from the junction with road 249D. This brings you to a meadow alongside a creek at an elevation of 8,862 shown on the topographic map.

Near the western end of this meadow, hike south up an old logging road that takes you part way up the mountain. Nearing the top, you must maneuver around some cliffs on the western side of the summit. Above the cliffs, you get to a flat summit area that offers no view. We returned right of the ascent route on old logging roads that led out to road 249 somewhat east of the starting point. The walk back to the parking place is in a flat grassy meadow south of the road, making a nice mile and a half loop.

To get to the other Peak 9,320, which we termed "Tank Top," drive on forest road 249E that circles south and west of Big Lake. A good starting point for the hike is at 9,080 feet directly west of the lake and east of Tank Top. Our hiking route was west across a flat meadow which was somewhat wet in mid-May. After crossing a fence, the route is a gradual ascent through open forest. As you may already have guessed, there is a water tank on top. The high point is a rocky outcrop south of the tank and offers limited views.

Our descent was on a winding road circling south and east down the mountain from the tank. This route brought us out behind a locked gate and signs "No Vehicles, No Camping" near our starting point of the two-mile hike.

S U Knolls are near Crescent Lake, a large lake a couple of miles north of Big Lake. The highest knoll of S U Knolls, at 9,419 feet, is east of Crescent Lake.

Drive to the road junction east of Crescent Lake, where Arizona 273 makes a sharp loop back to the north. This point can be reached from Arizona 260, either from three miles west of Eagar or from farther west in the Fort Apache Indian Reservation. At the junction east of Crescent Lake, forest road 113 runs on south to Big Lake. Park near this junction, which shows a 9,093 elevation point on the topographic map.

Hike east up the gradual slope, first through a grassy area and then through scattered trees to the high point. There are good views of Crescent Lake and the other knolls on the way up, but there is little view from the summit. The hike is a mile with an elevation gain of 350 feet.

Peak 9,880 is called "Burro Mountain" on the Apache-Sitgreaves National Forests map. The mountain is several miles northwest of Big Lake. Drive west on road 113 from the junction at S U Knolls. Go almost two miles west of the intersection of road 116 with road 113. This brings you to another road leading south from just west of a point shown as "BM 9366" on the topographic map. This point can be reached from the west by driving from Greer or from Arizona 273 as it leaves Arizona 260 in the Fort Apache Indian Reservation. The summit of Burro Mountain is at the western end of a broad massif that lies to the south of road 113. A poor-quality road leads from road 113 across the eastern flank of the mountain, but it is best to begin the hike from the junction on the main road.

Walk south up the road from the junction, passing through a gate. Hike along the road until it begins to level out into a broad saddle at 9,720 feet. Leave the road on the right and bushwhack west. You can bypass a small ridge point and then climb over a wide false summit before making the final climb to the high point. The summit is not easy to locate in the thick forest and there is no view from the top.

Pay careful attention to orientation after you leave the roadway — something we didn't. There are other roads on top of this broad-based mountain, which can make it confusing to get back to the starting point. The three-mile hike has an elevation gain of six hundred feet.

■

26

Loco Knoll; Peak 9,071; Peak 9,185; and Turner View

Rocky top of Loco Knoll.

General description: Three short gradual climbs to four summits
Hiking distances: Three hikes of 1 to 3 miles each
Starting elevations: 8,650 to 8,760 feet
High points: 9,069 to 9,185 feet
Elevation gains: 400 to 900 feet per hike
Maps: 7.5 minute Loco Knoll;
15 minute Alpine;
Apache-Sitgreaves National Forests

.

These four summits in the eastern part of the White Mountains can be visited from a loop auto trip from US 666. Climbing the four summits provides varied hiking over rocky slopes, through vast meadows, and in open forests.

From US 666 between Springerville and Nutrioso, drive east on Apache County road 116. This county road leaves US 666 a little over a mile south of Nelson Reservoir. Turn left after driving 1.4 miles on the county road and drive another four and a half miles to an intersection in a broad 8,630-foot saddle. Turn right at the intersection and park before the road begins to climb. Loco Knoll is a half mile southwest.

For a scenic two-mile loop hike, walk a mile south up the road to an 8,810-foot high point on the ridge south of Loco Knoll. Just as the road begins to descend, turn right, leave the road, and gradually climb through volcanic rock on the forested slope. A little rock scrambling brings you to the 9,069-foot high point in the extreme northeastern end of the summit area. The total ascent is 450 feet. A good return back to the starting point can be made by descending right of the rocky ridge that extends east from the summit.

Drive four and a half miles back to county road 116 and turn left, assuming you next want to climb Peaks 9,071 and 9,185. Drive on what is now forest road 275 until you reach a junction with road 851. Turn left on road 851 and park within a quarter of a mile, at an elevation of 8,680 feet.

Hike northeast across a large grassy meadow, aiming for the 9,071-foot summit, the right-hand or eastern one of the two distinctive summits to the north. Climb through scattered timber to the summit, which offers a partially open view.

Descend west to an 8,760-foot saddle and climb to the 9,185-foot summit, staying left of some obvious cliffs. A peek-a-boo view of the valley below is offered from the top. Make a direct descent south to the starting point by following a gradual route through the timber. The hike to the two summits is three miles with an elevation gain of nine hundred feet.

Drive a quarter-mile back west to forest road 275. Turn left and drive south on road 275 2.4 miles to a junction with road 577 which enters from the east. Park just south of this junction if you plan to climb Peak 9,143, which we call "Turner View."

Hike southeast through open timber, following various abandoned overgrown roads, to get to the summit of Turner View. This summit offers a good close-up view of Turner Peak, southeast just over the state line in New Mexico. The hike is a mile with four hundred feet of elevation gain.

■

27

Escudilla Mountain

Escudilla Mountain.

General description: A fine hike on old vehicle tracks
and trails to a lookout tower, followed by a walk through
the forest to the high point
Hiking distance: 8 miles
Starting elevation: 9,800 feet
High point: 10,912 feet
Elevation gain: 1,500 feet
Maps: 7.5 minute Alpine;
Apache-Sitgreaves National Forests

.

E scudilla Mountain is the high point of the eastern
   portion of the White Mountains. It is a distinctive,
stand-alone mountain with a double summit. The
lower southern portion of the summit area has a
lookout tower at 10,876 feet. The high point of 10,912
feet is over a half mile north of the lookout tower.
While there is a good trail to the lookout tower, the
route through the forest to the high point requires
some bushwhacking. It is a good hike to go just to the
lookout tower for those not interested in getting to the
high point.

Drive on US 666 and 180 between Alpine and
Nutrioso. A little north of midway between these two
towns, and two miles north of Alpine Divide, find
forest road 56 leading east. Drive about two miles
northeast on road 56 to a junction, where you take the
right fork toward Terry Flat. Drive generally east on
this right fork for approximately three miles to a
trailhead just beyond Toolbox Draw. The road to the
trailhead is not shown on either the U.S.G.S. or
national forest map.

Hike north on the trail that starts as an old vehicle
track. The trail follows the ridge east of Toolbox Draw.
Within a mile, the trail crosses the east end of Profanity
Ridge and makes a slight descent. The trail crosses a
meadow and then climbs gradually. The route bends to
the west as it approaches the lookout tower. For the
best views, you will need to climb the lookout tower.

To reach the high point of Escudilla Mountain, hike
north from the lookout tower. Descend through the
timber. There are a few helpful paths, but some
bushwhacking is required through the thick timber.

The descent is only eighty feet, after which there is a gradual climb to the 10,912-foot summit. The view from the high point is not nearly as good as the view from the lookout tower.

■

28

Thick Top; Peak 9,000;
and Peak 9,254

•

General description: Three short climbs to wooded summits
Hiking distances: Three hikes of one-half to one mile each
Starting elevations: 8,600 to 9,880 feet
High points: 9,000 to 10,092 feet
Elevation gains: 200 to 500 feet per hike
Maps: 15 minute Alpine;
    Apache-Sitgreaves National Forests

•

Peak 10,092 is the highest unnamed summit in the
Apache National Forest. A road that leads along the
flank of the peak makes the climb one of the shortest
hikes to a high summit. The short climb is not easy
through the heavy timber, and that is why we call this
summit "Thick Top." The other two summits also can
be reached by short climbs from nearby roads.

Drive east from US 666 and 180 on forest road 56 as
in the hike to Escudilla Mountain, hike #27. From the
road just west of the trailhead for the Escudilla Mountain hike, a loop road circles south around Terry Flat.
Thick Top is southwest of the southern portion of
Terry Flat. Drive in either direction around the loop
road to a parking place at 9,880 feet east of Thick Top.
    The climb of Thick Top is only a half-mile round trip
with just over two hundred feet of elevation gain, but
it seems farther. Bushwhack west to the high point.

There is a lot of downed timber in the forest that must be negotiated on the steep climb to the summit. There is not much view from the top, so the shortness of the climb is its only redeeming feature.

Peak 9,000 is west of forest road 56, only a mile from the highway. The best starting point is slightly north of a point directly east of the peak, at 8,600 feet. The climb of only a half-mile is through the timber west to the obvious high point.

Peak 9,254 is located midway between Peak 9,000 and Escudilla Mountain. The approach is from a spur road that leads north and east from the road to Terry Flat. As the Terry Flat road turns east, find a road leading northeast and then make a turn east within a quarter-mile. This brings you to a point, at 8,760 feet, south of Peak 9,254. Hike across a narrow meadow and continue north up through the trees to the summit. The hike of a mile gains five hundred feet of elevation.

■

29

Noble Mountain; Peak 9,507; Valley View Peak; and Noble View Peak

View point at the summit of Peak 9,507.

General description: Four hikes through the timber, with some hiking on logging roads and some through areas of logging debris
Hiking distances: Four hikes of 1 to 6 miles each
Starting elevations: 8,760 to 9,080 feet
High points: 9,080 to 9,585 feet
Elevation gains: 350 to 1,000 feet per hike
Maps: 15 minute Alpine;
    Apache-Sitgreaves National Forests

•

These four summits are northwest of Alpine and west of Alpine Divide. Two of the hikes are rather long for hikes to summits in this area. Much of the hiking is through areas of logging, requiring some route-finding skills.

The hikes to Noble Mountain and Peak 9,507 start from the same point but go in opposite directions. To get to the starting point, drive north from Alpine on US 666 and 180 almost two miles. Turn west on forest road 249 and go four and one-half miles to a junction with road 81. Turn right on road 81 and drive north a mile and one-half to a minor saddle. Park here, at an elevation of 9,080 feet.

Noble Mountain has an impressive name, but it doesn't qualify as a separate summit under the 300-foot rule. For the hike to Noble Mountain, walk east over a small knoll and climb through some logging debris. Bear left and climb northeast along the fence line. The hiking is slow through much downed timber, but the 9,480-foot summit is not hard to find. There is no view. The hike is two miles with a five-hundred-foot elevation gain.

The hike to Peak 9,507 is longer, five miles round trip with an elevation gain of eight hundred feet. The route follows the ridge west and north from the parking place. Start up the ridge west and northwest, following logging roads where possible. Stay close to the ridge crest as it bends to the north. Try to overcome the confusion of old and new logging roads. This route enables you to see first-hand the devastation of logging operations, and the massive amount of debris and trash that is left behind. We found this logging trash

Looking down
the valley from
Valley View
Peak.

much harder to hike through than the unlogged forest.
After descending from a false summit, you cross a
small meadow and then climb to the true summit.

The summit offers a good view east to Peak 9,585
across the valley. By adroit maneuvering you can see
Noble Mountain and the road over the pass where you
started this hike.

The entry point for the hike to the other two peaks
is Alpine Divide. From this divide, four miles north of
Alpine on US 666 and 180, drive west on a forest road
that curves around the right side of a ridge. Drive a
mile and a quarter on this road as it bends around to
the south and brings you to a flat saddle. This saddle
is between Peak 9,080, which we call "Valley View
Peak," and Peak 9,585, which we dubbed "Noble View
Peak." Park in the saddle at 8,760 feet.

To get to Valley View Peak, walk northeast on an old
vehicle track. There are many confusing roads, but
generally hike along the ridge as it bends north. The

high point is at the extreme northwest end of the almost flat summit area. The summit has cliffs to the west and a spectacular view of the valley to the north. The round trip is only a mile with 350 feet of climbing.

Return to the saddle for the climb to Noble View Peak. The route to Noble View Peak is a continuation of the road that brought you from the highway to this saddle. While many vehicles can be driven farther along this road, its quality deteriorates enough for us to consider the saddle a good starting point for this hike. If you start at the saddle, the hike is six miles with a thousand-foot elevation gain.

Walk west along the road as it climbs to the ridge crest. Bear right and continue to hike along another road. When this road descends right toward the valley, leave the road and continue north along the ridge. When you get to the area of the summit, the exact high point still is not easy to find. The summit of Noble View Peak appears to be the spot with a good view, with cliffs to the west and south. There is an outstanding view southwest to Noble Mountain and also a pleasing view west across the valley to Peak 9,507.

■

30

Tenney Mountain; Flat Top; Alpine View Peak; and Timber Top

■

General description: A varied group of hikes, with some
　walking on trails, some hiking in open country,
　and some bushwhacking and route-finding
Hiking distances: Four hikes of 1 to 4 miles each
Starting elevations: 8,559 to 9,200 feet
High points: 9,000 to 9,560 feet
Elevation gains: 200 to 1,100 feet per hike
Maps: 15 minute Alpine;
　Apache-Sitgreaves National Forests

■

T hese four summits are south and southwest of
　Alpine. For at least two of them, locating the
summit may be more of a problem than the hike itself.

　Tenney Mountain is an obscure, named point in a
large almost-flat area. Drive roughly three miles south
of Alpine on US 666 to forest road 403 that leads west.
Road 403 follows a different route than the one shown
on the national forest map. As you drive west on road
403, note the high ridge across the valley to the left.
The high point on this ridge is Tenney Mountain. After
driving about four miles west on road 403, find a
vehicle track that leads south down to the creek. Park
near this junction which is at an elevation of about
8,700 feet.
　Walk on the vehicle track down to the creek and bear

to the left. Hike east on the north side of the creek.
Find a logging road that leads uphill on the south side
of the creek. We can't describe an exact route because
there are so many ways to go. In any case, you must
climb generally south and southeast to locate the
9,058-foot high point. There is no view from the
wooded top. The hike is four miles with a six-hundred-
foot elevation gain.

A 9,560-foot summit we call "Flat Top" offers a
scenic trail hike starting from the highway. There may
be easier ways to get to the summit, but this trail hike
is most appealing. Drive south of Alpine on US 666
some two and a half miles to the point where the
highway turns sharply from west to southeast. This is
the point indicated by "BM 8559" on the topographic
map. Find a parking place along a vehicle track that
starts northwest up a valley.
Hike northwest on the vehicle track that soon
becomes a good trail. Follow this trail as it bears west
and comes out into a broad meadow. Leave the trail in
a flat area, bear right, and circle back to the east. Cross
a good-quality road and enter a flat forested area. The
problem then is to find the high point. You will see
why we call this one Flat Top. The summit is near the
southeastern part of the expansive level forested area.
Trial and error may be needed to find the summit as
you wander about on the forested top. The hike is four
miles with eleven hundred feet of elevation gain.

The summit we call "Alpine View Peak" has an
elevation of 9,000 feet. Drive a mile farther south on
US 666 to forest road 59E. Drive almost a mile east on
road 59E to the junction with road 59. Park here at
8,600 feet. Alpine View Peak is northwest of this
junction.
Hike northwest, staying left of a fence line. There is

downed timber and bushes to pass through as you get higher. Near the top, cross the fence to the right to get to the high point. To get the view of Alpine from Alpine View Peak, look through an opening in the trees just north of the summit. Return the way you came to complete the one-mile hike.

The next summit, at 9,400 feet, is one we call "Timber Top." Drive a mile east and southeast on road 59E from your parking place at the junction. Turn left and drive north and northeast on a good-quality logging road. Park within a quarter-mile. This puts you within a half-mile of the summit of Timber Top at an elevation of 9,200 feet.

Walk east, finding your way around large trees and much downed timber toward the hard-to-find high point of Timber Top. The summit is near the edge where steep cliffs drop off to the east. There is little view from the top.

■

31

Reno Lookout; Renos Neighbor; Peak 9,400; High Point; and Salt Benchmark

Reno Lookout.

General description: Two drives and three short
  off-trail hikes
Hiking distances: Three hikes of 1 mile each
Starting elevations: 8,840 to 9,360 feet
High points: 9,121 to 9,480 feet; drives to 9,094 and 9,184 feet
Elevation gains: 100 to 300 feet per hike
Maps: 15 minute Hannagan Meadow;
  Apache-Sitgreaves National Forests

High point of
Greenlee
County.

T hese five summits are in the Hannagan Meadow
area. One is the high point of Greenlee County.
Three of the summits can be visited by short walks and
two can be reached by vehicle.

Reno Lookout is served by forest road 25 that leaves
US 666 about five miles south of Hannagan Meadow.
Drive generally west on road 25 nearly six winding
miles to road 25C, a spur road to the right. Follow
road 25C to the lookout tower, which is at an elevation
of 9,094 feet. Reno Lookout provides a fine view, but it
is not a true summit, being a ridge point west of a
9,121-foot high point we call "Renos Neighbor."
If you wish to climb Renos Neighbor after visiting
Reno Lookout, return to forest road 25 and drive back
east almost two miles. East of Renos Neighbor, look for
an old logging road climbing directly west. Park here at
8,840 feet for the one-mile hike.
Walk west along the old roadbed and then bear right
to climb up the hill. The forested top of Renos Neighbor
is scarred by numerous logging tracks and there is little
view.

Approach Peak 9,400 from forest road 576 which

Start of the nature trail near Salt benchmark.

leaves US 666 at the northern edge of Hannagan Meadow. Drive road 576 as it winds northwest a little over two miles to a high point that shows an elevation 9,361 on the topographic map. From a little east of this point, walk north through the flat forested area. Climb gradually and search for the high point in the woods. This flattish summit offers no view. The one-mile hike has an elevation gain of less than a hundred feet.

We call the next summit "High Point," because it is the highest point in Greenlee County. Drive south from Hannagan Meadow on US 666 three and a half miles to a stretch of highway that runs north and south. Find a parking place at 9,360 feet near a vehicle track that leads east.

Walk east up the vehicle track a quarter mile. Bear off to the right and climb gradually through the trees. Cross a fence and enter a vast flat open area. Walk through the scattered vegetation to locate the high point, somewhat to the southeast. There are some rock outcrops which we took to be the 9,480-foot top. The trip is only a mile with an elevation gain of 150 feet.

Salt benchmark is a couple of miles farther south along US 666. You can drive to the benchmark and also take a walk on a short nature trail. Drive to the spur road leading west from US 666 marked as the starting point for the Blue Vista Nature Trail. At the parking area, it takes a little searching to find the U.S.G.S. marker for Salt benchmark. It is located on the west edge of the parking area. The benchmark, at 9,184 feet, is not a summit.

A walk from the parking area on the nature trail will take you to slightly lower elevations. As well as the nature trail, there are picnic facilities near the Salt benchmark parking area.

■

32

Blue Peak

.

General description: A hike on a closed roadway and
a fine foot trail
Hiking distance: 8 miles
Starting elevation: 9,080 feet
High point: 9,346 feet
Elevation gain: 800 feet
Maps: 15 minute Hannagan Meadow;
Apache-Sitgreaves National Forests

.

B lue Peak is the southernmost summit above
nine-thousand feet in the White Mountains.
Consequently, its lookout tower provides a fine view of
the rolling country south and east. Blue Peak is served
by a five-mile road plus a little over a mile of trail.
Recently, the lookout tower on Blue Peak has not been
used, so the road entry may not be maintained well
enough to permit driving to the trailhead. If not, you
can enjoy a longer hike through this beautiful area.
The figures in the heading assume you will be able to
drive halfway on the road section, about the amount
we were able to drive on our trip.

Take US 666 to about six miles south of Hannagan
Meadow, where forest road 84 leads east. This road is
two hundred yards north of the road to Blue Vista
Nature Trail. How far you will be able to drive east on

road 84 will depend on current road conditions. Walk east to the end of the road, finally descending to 8,840 feet. Here a fine foot trail begins. The trail, in the Blue Range Primitive Area, makes one long switchback as it climbs to the 9,346-foot summit of Blue Peak.

Blue Peak was given its name in 1969. The older topographic map indicates a benchmark and lookout. The tower at Blue Peak gives splendid views because it overlooks the vast area to the south and east.

■

Southeastern Ranges

The southeastern mountain ranges of Arizona emerge as independent high areas extending far above the desert floor. Of the sixteen ranges covered in this section, five rise above nine thousand feet. The highest, the Pinaleno Mountains, reach 10,720 feet at the summit of Mount Graham.

Climbing the high summits in the southeastern area presents a wide range of hiking and climbing difficulty. There are fine trail hikes to high summits in the Chiricahua, Huachuca, Santa Rita, Rincon, and Galiuro Mountains. Easy off-trail hikes will take you to the top of ranges such as the Swisshelm, Mule, and Patagonia Mountains. Several other ranges, the Winchester, Whetstone, and Dragoon Mountains, have high points that are much harder to reach, requiring brushy bushwhacks and rock scrambles. The high point of the Baboquivari Mountains is the most difficult to climb, requiring technical climbing equipment and skills.

There are four high summits that are accessible by automobile. Mount Lemmon in the Santa Catalina Mountains has a ski area near the top. The three other summits with roads to the top are in the Pinaleno Mountains.

33

Pinnacle Ridge

Pinnacle Ridge.

General description: A moderately long hike and a
   strenuous climb, with bushwhacking and rock scrambling
Hiking distance: 10 miles
Starting elevation: 5,480 feet
High point: 7,550 feet
Elevation gain: 3,000 feet
Maps: 7.5 minute Buford Hill (essential);
   Coronado National Forest (Santa Teresa Mountains)

.

T he Santa Teresa Mountains form an isolated range west of Safford and southeast of Globe. The northern portion of the Santa Teresa Mountains is in the San Carlos Indian Reservation while the southern part is in Coronado National Forest. The high point of the range is Mount Turnbull at 8,282 feet in the reservation. The high point in the Coronado National Forest part of the range is on spectacular Pinnacle Ridge, which is in the Santa Teresa Wilderness and is a challenging and complex climb.

Getting to the trailhead requires a long but scenic drive on backroads. The entry point is from a secondary road that leads southwest from US 70 fifteen miles northwest of Safford. This good-quality road is shown on the maps, but is unnamed and unnumbered. Drive from US 70 on this road some twenty miles to road 677. Follow road 677 which leads northeast of a hill on which you can see a microwave tower. The junction with road 677 can be reached from the south by driving the Aravaipa Road northwest from Bonita.

Road 677 leads two winding miles northwest from the main road to a junction near a gate northeast of a little knoll called Oak Butte. As road 677 turns north, a rugged jeep track leads southwest beyond the gate. This jeep track, which is impassable to almost all vehicles, is the route toward Pinnacle Ridge. It is two miles from the start of the jeep track at the gate to the national forest boundary.

The entire area along the main road, road 677, and the jeep track to the national forest boundary is state land. It would be necessary to drive all the way to the forest boundary to avoid parking on state land (see introduction). Nevertheless, numerous parties have been using the area at the start of the jeep track for parking and camping in order to climb Pinnacle Ridge. The figures in the heading assume you start hiking here.

The hiking route first goes southwest along the jeep track and then turns northwest as it descends into Buford Canyon. The track pulls out of the canyon on the left soon thereafter. The route goes north, climbs over Blue Ridge, and descends to Devils Hole. Near the crest of Blue Ridge you reach the national forest boundary and soon thereafter you enter the Santa Teresa Wilderness. Shortly beyond the wilderness boundary, you get to Devils Hole.

At Devils Hole, pass left of Devil Tank. Bear left and hike north up the valley, following some dozer tracks as far as they go. Then pick a route left of the main drainage that will take you north and northwest to the top of the ridge. While there is some bushwhacking, a fairly open route can be found most of the way. On the ridge crest you should be in or left of a 6,780-foot saddle.

Turn left and hike west up the ridge. At the 7,200-foot level, stay right of two prominent rock pinnacles. Carefully work right around the base of the higher pinnacle. Circle left of the next pinnacle, which is the high point, and spiral around to its northwest side. From this side the climb is southeast over large boulders. There is a little exposure on the final scramble to the top of the highest summit rock.

The view from the rocky cap of Pinnacle Ridge is unobstructed. Nearby you can see the many spectacular rock pinnacles along the ridge. In the distance you have enchanting views of many other southern Arizona mountain ranges.

■

34

Bassett Peak

■

General description: A fine trail hike
Hiking distance: 12 miles
Starting elevation: 4,880 feet
High point: 7,663 feet
Elevation gain: 3,000 feet
Maps: 7.5 minute Harrison Canyon;
7.5 minute Bassett Peak;
Coronado National Forest (Galiuro Mountains)

■

B assett Peak is the high point of the Galiuro Mountains. Most of the Galiuros are not accessible enough for practical day hikes, and the excellent trail system in the Galiuro Wilderness makes this prime backpacking country. Bassett Peak, however, is near enough to a trailhead to make the climb a suitable day hike.

The approach is from the east side of the range via Ash Creek. The road to the trailhead gradually deteriorates, so the amount of walking on the road will depend on your vehicle. From Willcox on Interstate 10, drive north on the Fort Grant Road. After making several right angle turns and driving twenty-two miles, turn left and drive west on road 651. Drive generally west about fifteen miles and turn left onto forest road 660 just after entering the Coronado National Forest.

Pass through a gate and drive west. Most cars can drive a mile, so we will assume that this mile will take you to the starting point for the hike.

Hike west to the end of the road and then continue west on a trail. The trail proceeds up the Ash Creek valley, climbs north to a spur ridge, and finally tops out on the main ridge crest. At a trail junction at 6,900 feet on the ridge crest turn left and follow the trail south along the ridge. After a little over a mile, the trail bears right of the ridge and climbs up the west side of Bassett Peak. The main trail goes on past the peak, but you can find well-beaten paths for the short distance to the summit.

Bassett Peak is the southernmost high point of the Galiuro Mountains. You can see the main part of the range extending northward, with a number of summits almost as high. There are grandiose views in other directions as well.

■

35

Reiley Peak

.

General description: An arduous climb with bushwhacking
and rock scrambling
Hiking distance: 8 miles
Starting elevation: 4,900 feet
High point: 7,631 feet
Elevation gain: 2,800 feet
Maps: 7.5 minute Reiley Peak (essential);
Coronado National Forest (Winchester Mountains)

.

T he Winchester Mountains are northwest of Willcox.
The small national forest area has no maintained
trails, and the road approaches are long drives from
the highway. Although the country is wild and
beautiful, many people may not really enjoy the climb
of Reiley Peak because of the difficult bushwhacking
and rock scrambling. The tedious climb is much harder
than the figures in the heading imply.

There are several possible approaches to Reiley Peak,
all of which are reported to be difficult. One approach
is to drive north from Interstate 10 at Willcox on the
Fort Grant Road. After nineteen miles, as the main
road turns north, continue west on road 690. Follow
this narrow section-line road six miles west and then
curve south a mile to the forest boundary. A high
clearance vehicle may be a necessity to make it to the

forest boundary under most conditions. It is best to park inside the national forest, as the access road comes through private property. Just inside the gate at the boundary there is a small stock pond on the left in a level area. Park here.

The hiking route is generally south and southwest to Reiley Peak. Hike south on the vehicle track as it goes up the east side of Reiley Canyon. Within a half mile, bear right, cross the canyon, and climb southwest up the nose of an open ridge. Pass by a 5,842-foot ridge point and climb more steeply west through an increasingly brushy area. Contour left at the 6,500-foot level to bypass a striking 6,684-foot rocky ridge point. Cross west through a 6,500-foot saddle and climb west and southwest to the ridge crest at 7,300 feet. Bear left and hike south up the ridge to the summit.

Whichever route you take to Reiley Peak, we feel sure you will encounter most of the hazards of desert mountain climbing, such as cactus, catclaw, steep rock slopes, and thick brush. Once on top, however, there is a feeling of satisfaction for reaching this difficult summit.

If you found a good route on the way up, it is best to follow the same route back. It is tempting to descend east from the summit, but it is easy to get cliffed out or find thicker brush on such a descent route.

■

36

Eagle Rock; Heliograph Peak; Plain View Peak; Hawk Peak; and Mount Graham

.

General description: Three short hikes on trail and easy
off-trail routes to named high points and
two summit drives
Hiking distances: Three hikes of one-half to two miles each
Starting elevations: 8,980 to 10,500 feet
High points: 9,380 to 10,627 feet; drives to 10,022
and 10,720 feet
Elevation gains: 100 to 500 feet per hike
Maps: 7.5 minute Mount Graham;
7.5 minute Webb Peak;
Coronado National Forest (Pinaleno Mountains)

.

T he Pinaleno Mountains comprise the highest
mountain range in southeastern Arizona and the
third highest in the state. There are ten named summits
above nine thousand feet in the Pinalenos, topped by
Mount Graham at 10,720 feet. A paved road leads
much of the way up the mountain and a good road
traverses the flattish top of the range.

There is confusion on terminology concerning the
Pinaleno Mountains, some of which is compounded by
signs in the area. The Pinaleno Mountains are sometimes referred to as "The Grahams." Mount Graham,
the high point of the Pinaleno Mountains often is
called "High Peak."

Three of the summits in the Pinalenos can be
reached by road while each of the other seven requires

a short hike. It would be possible to get to all ten summits in a long day, but at least two days are suggested for maximum pleasure in visiting the ten summits. This chapter covers the five summits on the eastern part of the range, a trip that makes a comfortable day's outing.

Drive on US 666 between Interstate 10 and Safford. Turn west on Arizona 366, which leaves US 666 seven miles south of Safford. Drive this winding paved road west up the mountain range. After twenty-one miles of driving from US 666, you reach a junction with two roads on the right. One leads up to Heliograph Peak and the other descends to Shannon Campground. The hike to Eagle Rock starts from the campground at 8,980 feet.

Hike east on the trail that leaves the south side of the campground. After a level half mile, the trail climbs another half mile on switchbacks to a saddle on the ridge south of Heliograph Peak. From this saddle at 9,340 feet, Eagle Rock is on the left only fifty yards away and forty feet higher. Leave the trail on the left and work your way around and over large boulders to get to the highest rock. The unobstructed view east and southeast from the summit is one of the best in the Pinaleno Mountains.

The trail to the saddle near Eagle Rock does not follow the route shown on the topographic map. The trail crosses the 9,340-foot saddle near Eagle Rock rather than the 9,500-foot saddle higher up the ridge. The trail continues past Eagle Rock and descends to Arcadia Campground, while a spur trail climbs a mile to Heliograph Peak.

Continue on the spur trail that starts just across the saddle if you want to hike to Heliograph Peak. If you prefer, you can drive to the top. A road climbs two miles to the 10,022-foot summit from the intersection at the road entering Shannon Campground. A lookout tower on the summit of Heliograph Peak can provide unobstructed views.

A half mile beyond the intersection with the roads to Shannon Campground and Heliograph Peak, a road leads north to Mount Graham. You can drive all the way to Mount Graham and you can climb two other summits from the Mount Graham road. Some three miles up the winding road toward Mount Graham, the road makes a sharp loop to the east. Plain View Peak is northeast of this road loop.

Hike northeast from the road less than a quarter of a mile to the 10,370-foot summit of Plain View Peak. The hike takes you up only a hundred vertical feet through the open timber. Despite its name, the summit of Plain View Peak doesn't offer much of a view.

Continue the drive toward Mount Graham for another half mile. Find a side road branching off to the left. Park here for the hike to Hawk Peak.

Walk northwest along the side road a half mile as the road descends slightly from the starting elevation of 10,500 feet. You reach a saddle at 10,460 feet east of Hawk Peak. As the road bears left and continues to descend, leave the road on the right and climb west through the timber. A half mile of gradual climbing brings you to the tree-covered 10,627-foot summit of Hawk Peak.

From the intersection at the start of the hike to Hawk Peak, the drive is less than a mile farther to the top of Mount Graham. At this writing, the summit area is covered with experimental equipment, so you must search out the high point of 10,720 feet:

The future for the top of Mount Graham currently is under study and there no doubt will be development for its use as an observatory site. Thus, the access to the top of Mount Graham may be different in the future. We can only hope that development will be handled in such a way as to permit visiting the high point of Mount Graham and each of the other summits in the Pinaleno Mountains.

■

Clark Peak; Merrill Peak; Grand View Peak; Webb Peak; and Grant Hill

On the summit of Merrill Peak.

■

General description: A hike on trail, three short walks through the forest, and a drive to a lookout tower

Hiking distances: Four hikes of 1 to 2 miles each

Starting elevations: 8,985 to 9,313 feet

High points: 9,006 to 9,660 feet; drive to 10,030 feet

Elevation gains: 300 to 500 feet per hike

Maps: 7.5 minute Webb Peak;
Coronado National Forest

.

T hese five summits are in the western part of the Pinaleno Mountains. A drive to a lookout tower and four short hikes make a reasonable day's outing.

Drive to the top of the Pinaleno Mountains as in hike #36. Continue west on the main road, called the Swift Trail, until the road ends. The trailhead parking area at the end of the road is a little over a mile beyond the side road going south to Riggs Lake.

The trail west from the road end is the route to Clark Peak. From the start at 8,985 feet the trail descends to a saddle at 8,780 feet and then climbs along the south side of Clark Peak, all in less than a mile. After reaching a high point in the trail, leave the trail on the right and climb through the timber eighty vertical feet in a hundred yards to the 9,006-foot wooded summit.

For the climb of Merrill Peak, drive back east three-quarters of a mile beyond the road turning south to Riggs Lake. Park at the extreme south end of a sharp loop in the road at an elevation of 9,140 feet.

Hike south and southeast on a trail for a quarter of a mile to a trail junction. Take the right fork southwest a couple of hundred yards to a saddle. Leave the trail on the right as the trail bends south and continue south-west over a small rise and into a meadow in a saddle. Climb more steeply through the timber directly west to the 9,288-foot summit. Near the summit, there is an excellent view to the southwest from some rock outcrops.

For the hike to Grand View Peak, drive almost a mile farther east along the main road. Park where a jeep trail goes left (north) at an elevation of 9,313 feet shown on the topographic map.

Walk north up the jeep trail and immediately take a right-forking vehicle track that climbs northeast. Follow this track to its end and then climb through the trees to the summit. The southern summit, the first one reached, is higher at 9,660 feet than the 9,618-foot point to the north. Despite its name, there is little view from Grand View Peak.

You can drive to the summit of Webb Peak under good conditions. Return east on the main road slightly over two miles to forest road 88 leading north to Webb Peak. A drive of two more miles on this side road brings you to the high summit with its lookout tower. Webb Peak at 10,030 feet is the high point in the western part of the Pinaleno Mountains.

Grant Hill is a wooded high point south of Mount Graham. It is south of the main road and is surrounded by a conglomeration of old roads and vehicle tracks. The starting point is at Hospital Flat. If you are returning east from Webb Peak, drive back to the Hospital Flat Campground area. This is a little over a mile west of the road going north to Mount Graham. Find a side road leading south just west of Hospital Flat, where the main road makes a loop to the south.

Hike south on any of several vehicle tracks and bear right to climb southwest up the gradual slope through the forest. Vehicle tracks should get you halfway to the top on the mile hike to the high point, with an elevation gain of three hundred feet. Don't expect to see much but the surrounding trees from this flat 9,477-foot wooded summit.

■

38

Mount Lemmon

.

General description: A long, winding, scenic drive on
    a paved road
Hiking distance: Optional
High point: 9,157 feet
Maps: 7.5 minute Mount Lemmon;
    Coronado National Forest (Santa Catalina Mountains)

.

M ount Lemmon, the high point of the Santa
Catalina Mountains, is the highest summit in
Arizona that can be reached by a paved highway. A ski
resort is near the top and observatories are on the
summit. The Santa Catalina Mountains have a wealth
of hiking trails for the hiker or backpacker who prefers
to travel on foot. The Pusch Ridge Wilderness covers a
portion of the Santa Catalina Mountains, but not the
high point at Mount Lemmon.

From Tucson, drive east on Tanque Verde Road to a
left turn onto the Catalina Highway. Follow this road
as it winds up through the Santa Catalina Mountains
past numerous lookout points to the ski area at 8,340
feet. Continue on the paved road beyond the ski area
parking lot. There is a gate just beyond the parking lot
that is sometimes locked if the road conditions require
it. It is two more miles to the summit. If you drive to
the end of the road, the only walking will be amidst

the observatory buildings to find the true high point, which is at 9,157 feet.

For the long distance hiker or backpacker, a nineteen-mile trail route to Mount Lemmon starts at the Coronado National Forest Visitor's Center. It goes by way of Romero Pass. Other routes to the top start at the Catalina State Park west of the range. A runner has covered the route from the Visitor's Center to the summit in just less than three hours, but most hikers would consider it an exhausting all-day trip.

■

39

Mica Mountain

.

.

General description: An extremely long hike on good trail
    that many may prefer to make into a backpacking trip
Hiking distance: 26 miles
Starting elevation: 2,749 feet
High point: 8,664 feet
Elevation gain: 7,435 feet
Maps: 7.5 minute Tanque Verde Peak;
    7.5 minute Mica Mountain;
    Coronado National Forest (Rincon Mountains)

M ica Mountain is the high point of the Rincon
Mountains, which are east of Tucson. It is a
rounded, wooded summit remote from trailheads. Mica
Mountain is in the eastern section of Saguaro National
Monument. The Rincon Mountain Wilderness adjoins
the Saguaro National Monument on the east and
south. The Rincon Mountains have a sizeable roadless
area with fine trails and campsites which are popular
with backpackers.

The most straightforward approach for the hike to
Mica Mountain is from the west. Drive east from
Tucson on East Speedway Road until it ends at a paved
trailhead parking area.
Hike east on the trail, passing Douglas Spring Camp
in five and a half miles and reaching Cow Head Saddle

at 6,100 feet after a total of eight miles. During this stretch there are no side trails except a few horse paths. In Cow Head Saddle, you are at the low point between Mica Mountain on the left and Tanque Verde Peak on the right. Tanque Verde Peak is the high point of the Tanque Verde Mountains, which are commonly thought of as part of the Rincon Mountains. There is a junction of four trails at Cow Head Saddle. Take the left fork up the ridge toward Mica Mountain.

For the shortest route from Cow Head Saddle to Mica Mountain, turn sharply left on a climbing trail after three more miles, when the trail straight ahead goes to Manning Camp. The proper trail is found after you pass the huge rock outcrop of Helens Dome on the left and just after a level side trail on the left goes north on the east side of Helens Dome. At the junction where the right fork goes to Manning Camp, follow the climbing trail east to the summit.

The lookout tower on Mica Mountain, which had not been used for many years, has been removed. Without benefit of a view from the tower, you will have to be satisfied with views of the surrounding forest.

While top runners have completed the round trip from the end of Speedway Road to Mica Mountain in less than four hours, most hikers consider it a dawn to dusk effort. Backpackers should inquire about campsite reservations at the Saguaro National Monument headquarters.

There are shorter approaches to Mica Mountain from the north and from the southeast, but the trailheads are remote and require long drives on back roads.

■

40

Baboquivari Peak

Baboquivari Peak.

General description: A wearying route-finding hike to a high saddle, followed by bushwhacking and a three-pitch technical rock climb
Hiking distance: 8 miles
Starting elevation: 4,500 feet
High point: 7,734 feet
Elevation gain: 3,500 feet
Map: 7.5 minute Baboquivari Peak (essential)

The distinctive spire of Baboquivari Peak.

B aboquivari Peak is the distinctive spire that can be observed from many points in southeastern Arizona. Its climb is the most difficult of the routes described in this book. The ascent of Baboquivari Peak should only be attempted by parties led by those experienced in route finding and in technical climbing. While each of the three rock-climbing pitches can be free-climbed by experienced climbers, most hikers will want the security of a belay, particularly if conditions are less than ideal.

From Arizona 86 at Three Points, between Tucson and Sells, drive south on Arizona 286. After thirty miles, near milepost 17, turn west on an unpaved road. This road leads up Thomas Canyon to what formerly was Riggs Ranch and later was a Nature Conservancy facility. More recently, it was reported that the ranch is again privately owned. The road rapidly deteriorates after you leave the highway, so that a high-clearance vehicle, preferably one with four-wheel-drive, is needed to reach the trailhead.

If road conditions require a hike of several miles to the end of the road, a backpack trip is suggested. A backpack is particularly needed if your party expects to

The northern
approach to the
Baboquivari Peak
summit.

spend considerable time on roped climbing.

The road from the highway to the ranch passes
through both private land and state land. It is important to get permission if you intend to park or camp in
the area.

From the ranch buildings, get well oriented for the
hike to the saddle, which is north (right) of Baboquivari
Peak. Find a beaten path leading northwest up the
creek bed. Hike up the hard-to-follow path, staying
with the bottom of Thomas Canyon for a mile. The
path then pulls out on the hillside to the right. Now
easier to follow, the trail skirts right of the drainage
and eventually brings you to the saddle at 6,380 feet
on the ridge crest north of Baboquivari Peak.

Turn left and bushwhack southwest from the saddle
toward a higher minor saddle visible to the right of the
peak. Before you get to the minor saddle, you come to
the first rock-climbing pitch. A route to the right has
secure footholds, but there is considerable exposure. A
safer but more difficult route is up a wide crack to the

Free-climbing the second pitch on Baboquivari Peak.

left. Good belaying positions are above these pitches.

Continuing above the first pitch, work up around the west side of the summit to the second steep pitch. Climb this short steep section on knobby rock, the easiest of the three pitches.

Climb on up to the base of the third pitch, the longest and hardest one. This section can be particularly difficult if the rock is wet. While small ledges and cracks make for straightforward climbing, the length of the pitch, some sixty feet, warrants protection for all climbers.

Trudge up a well-beaten path from the top of the third pitch to the summit. The view from the top is unsurpassed. The flat rock-topped summit area gives no hint of the steep route from below. Both the saddle north of the peak and the summit are often used for overnight camping by backpackers.

While an ascent of Baboquivari Peak should only be attempted by experienced climbers, a successful climb can provide an exhilarating experience. Parties should

The start of the third pitch on Baboquivari Peak.

allow plenty of time, as a day hike can be a dawn to dusk effort even with a start at the ranch.

The crest of the Baboquivari Mountains forms the eastern boundary of the Tohono O'odham (formerly Papago) Indian Reservation. The approach from the east described here avoids the reservation except for perhaps a short stretch near the summit. A western approach that was formerly used, while reported to be somewhat easier, requires driving and hiking on the Indian Reservation. It is always wise to get permission before driving or hiking on Indian lands.

■

41

Mount Ian and Mount Wrightson

Mount Wrightson, with Mount Ian on the ridge to the left.

General description: A classic long hike on trail with a
very short off-trail portion
Hiking distance: 15 miles
Starting elevation: 5,420 feet
High point: 9,146 and 9,453 feet
Elevation gain: 4,700 feet
Maps: 7.5 minute Mount Hopkins (trailhead barely on edge);
7.5 minute Mount Wrightson;
Coronado National Forest (Santa Rita Mountains)

.

T he Santa Rita Mountains, one of the prime hiking areas of southeastern Arizona, have two summits above nine thousand feet. Both summits can be climbed in one long day hike into the Mount Wrightson Wilderness. Fine trails lead to Mount Wrightson, the highest summit of the range. Only a short ascent from one of these trails is needed to reach Mount Ian, Mount Wrightson's unofficially-named neighbor.

The trailhead is in Madera Canyon, on the north side of the Santa Rita Mountains. From Continental, a small settlement east of Green Valley, proceed thirteen miles southeast and south. Near the end of the road into Madera Canyon, take the left fork into a two-tiered parking area.

There are several trails to Mount Wrightson, a summit that is a favorite of veteran hikers. Hike south on an old roadbed from the upper level of the parking area. After 0.3 mile, turn sharply left at a trail junction and follow this trail to Josephine Saddle at 7,100 feet. Hike left on the trail up the ridge and stay left at two subsequent trail junctions to get to Baldy Saddle at 8,780 feet.

At Baldy Saddle, Mount Ian is to the north and Mount Wrightson to the south. To climb Mount Ian, turn left and follow the trail north a mile. After the trail rounds two ridges and begins to descend, leave the trail on the left. Bushwhack east through sparse vegetation, climbing two hundred yards to the 9,146-foot rocky summit.

Return to the junction with the ascent trail at Baldy Saddle. Hike south a few yards to another junction. Take the right fork at this junction and follow this trail. Climb a short but steep mile to the bare summit of

Mount Wrightson with its magnificent views. Mount Wrightson is said to be the best view point in the southeastern Arizona mountain ranges.

For a figure-eight loop trip, turn right near Baldy Saddle on the return and follow the longer Super Trail. The Super Trail circles south of Mount Wrightson and continues down from Josephine Saddle east of the trail used on the ascent. The Super Trail returns to the northeast corner of the parking lot.

■

42

Mount Washington

The ghost town of Duquesne.

■

General description: A hike along a vehicle track with an off-trail ascent through open forest
Hiking distance: 8 miles
Starting elevation: 5,310 feet
High point: 7,221 feet
Elevation gain: 2,200 feet
Maps: 7.5 minute Duquesne;
   Coronado National Forest (Patagonia Mountains)

Partial view from the summit of Mount Washington.

T he southernmost high summit in Arizona is Mount Washington, only a mile and a half north of the Mexican border. Mount Washington is the high point of the Patagonia Mountains. The open forested area makes for a straightforward ascent.

The starting point is at Duquesne, a ghost town some fifteen miles south of Patagonia. If approaching from Patagonia, follow forest roads 58 and 49 south to Duquesne. Park along the main road in the southern part of the ghost town, near a poor-quality side road leading west. This road crosses private property (see introduction) before it reaches the national forest.

Walk west on the rough road, keeping left as a right fork goes to a mine. Enter the Coronado National Forest through a gate after a mile. Continue another mile west, staying left of a drainage.

Near an intersection of vehicle tracks where one track goes north, turn left, leave the vehicle tracks and climb south through the timber. Gain the top of the ridge and turn right to follow the ridge crest west. Continue west and southwest along the timbered ridge until you reach the summit of Mount Washington at 7,221 feet.

A partial view south into Mexico can be gained from the summit area. There are two unnamed summits above seven thousand feet on the ridge running north and east from Mount Washington.

A venturesome hiker can make a good loop trip over these two summits on the return. Without a topographic map and a sure sense of direction, it is best to return the way you came.

■

43

Miller Peak and Carr Peak

Miller Peak from the summit of Carr Peak.

General description: Two moderate hikes on trail
Hiking distances: 9 and 5 miles
Starting elevations: 6,550 and 7,380 feet
High points: 9,466 and 9,237 feet
Elevation gains: 3,000 and 2,000 feet
Maps: 7.5 minute Montezuma Pass;
    7.5 minute Miller Peak;
    Coronado National Forest (Huachuca Mountains)

.

F ine trails abound in the Huachuca Mountains.
Some of the best trails lead to the two high points
above nine thousand feet. While the two peaks can be
climbed in one long day from any of several trailheads,
we suggest two separate hikes to better enjoy the
excellent hiking in the Huachuca Mountains. The
higher portion of the range is in the Miller Peak
Wilderness.

The hike to Miller Peak, the high point of the range,
begins at Montezuma Pass. Drive south from Sierra
Vista on Arizona 92 for fourteen miles. Just after
Arizona 92 turns to the east, turn right and drive south
on forest road 61. This road turns west and leads to
Montezuma Pass. Backroad approaches to Montezuma
Pass also can be made from Nogales, Patagonia, or
Sonoita.

From the large parking and rest area at Montezuma
Pass, cross the road and hike north on a good trail.
Follow the trail four miles to a junction at 9,125 feet.
Turn right and follow the switchbacking trail to the
9,466-foot summit.

The Huachuca Mountains form the third highest
mountain range in southeastern Arizona. Miller Peak,
with its lookout tower, provides unobstructed views far
south into Mexico.

We suggest an approach to Carr Peak from Carr
Canyon. Drive south from Sierra Vista on Arizona 92
for seven miles. Turn right on forest road 368. Follow
this road west and southwest as it climbs on many
switchbacks and ends at a trailhead parking area at
7,380 feet. Unless road improvements are made, a
high-clearance vehicle may be required to drive all the

way to the trailhead.

Hike up the trail that spirals east and south around Carr Peak. Southwest of the peak, at an elevation of almost nine thousand feet, find a spur trail on the right. Follow this spur trail northwest and then east to the rock-topped summit. Carr Peak, at 9,237 feet, towers over the surrounding area. It is higher than all but Miller Peak, across the valley to the south.

The two summits can be climbed together in a longer day from either of the trailheads described by using the trail system between the two peaks. Another approach for either or both peaks is from Miller Canyon, entered by driving east from Arizona 92 on forest road 56. From a trailhead at 5,740 feet, a good trail leads to a trail junction at Bathtub Spring, on the trail system midway between Miller Peak and Carr Peak.

■

44

Apache Peak

■

General description: A long rugged hike up a beautiful
　　canyon and through thick brush
Hiking distance: 10 miles
Starting elevation: 4,800 feet
High point: 7,711 feet
Elevation gain: 3,000 feet
Maps: 7.5 minute McGrew Spring;
　　7.5 minute Apache Peak (essential);
　　Coronado National Forest (Whetstone Mountains)

■

A pache Peak is the high point of the Whetstone
Mountains, a small isolated range in southeastern
Arizona. Because there are few trails and much difficult
terrain in this range, the Whetstones get little hiking
traffic. Nevertheless, there are beautiful canyons and
other attractions that make hiking in the Whetstones
worthwhile.

The best approach to Apache Peak is from the east
side of the range. Drive south on Arizona 90 from
Interstate 10 just west of Benson. In just over ten
miles, turn right on forest road 369 which leads to
French Joe Canyon. Stay left after three-quarters of a
mile as the road to the right goes to French Joe Camp.
The road deteriorates, but hopefully you can drive at
least a half mile farther to park inside the Coronado

National Forest boundary. If you are able to drive into the national forest, you will be parking on the south side of French Joe Canyon at 4,800 feet.

Walk west on the rough road that soon becomes just a vehicle track. Follow the track as far as it goes up the canyon and then continue to climb in the canyon bottom. Pass French Joe Spring at 5,180 feet as the canyon briefly turns southwest and then goes northwest. Depending on the season, pools and waterfalls may cause you to detour out of the canyon bottom; the right-hand side is usually best. When you reach a major canyon junction at 6,060 feet, take the right (northwest) fork. Soon thereafter, bear left or west out of the canyon. Maneuver through the brush northwest to Lone Pine Saddle. This flat overgrown saddle at 6,860 feet is on a ridge extending east from the main north-south spine of the Whetstone Mountains. As you face west from the saddle, Apache Peak is on the right and French Joe Peak, a ridge point almost as high, is southwest on the left.

Trudge west up the ridge from Lone Pine Saddle toward a ridge point between Apache Peak and French Joe Peak. After climbing to 7,400 feet, you can either continue up and over this ridge point or make a fairly difficult contour right to go around it. Either choice brings you to a saddle at 7,460 feet southeast of Apache Peak. From this broad saddle, climb northwest through trees and minor cliffs to the summit.

The summit of Apache Peak, at 7,711 feet, is open enough to give terrific views of the lower summits of the Whetstone Mountains as well as distant vistas of other mountain ranges.

While the ascent up French Joe Canyon makes a beautiful hike, the rock scrambling around the pools and waterfalls may be more difficult than some hikers prefer. We are told of an easier alternate route that leaves the canyon at 5,200 feet just west of French Joe

Spring. As the canyon turns to the northwest, climb out on the left to gain a ridge. Follow this ridge west and northwest over several minor ridge points to French Joe Peak at 7,675 feet. Then hike north to the 7,460-foot saddle and on up Apache Peak.

■

45

Mount Glenn

.

General description: A route-finding effort to a ridge,
   a steep ridge climb, and a final bushwhack
Hiking distance: 6 miles
Starting elevation: 4,760 feet
High point: 7,500 feet
Elevation gain: 3,000 feet
Maps: 7.5 minute Cochise Stronghold (essential);
   Coronado National Forest (Dragoon Mountains)

.

M ount Glenn, the high point of the Dragoon
   Mountains, is an undistinguished summit north
of the spectacular rock formations around Cochise
Stronghold. Mount Glenn can be approached by
several routes. A route from the east is described here.

From Interstate 10, drive south on US 666 to Sunsites.
Turn west on road 84, the road leading to Cochise
Stronghold. A good starting point for the hike is some
seven miles west of Sunsites, just after the road turns
south at the Coronado National Forest boundary. Find
a vehicle track leading northwest and park near this
side road.

Walk northwest along the vehicle track as it leads up
the southwest side of Carlink Canyon. When the
vehicle track runs out between the canyon and cliffs on
the left, bushwhack and scramble across the rugged

canyon. Climb north through open country to the crest of a ridge. Turn left and trudge west up this open ridge. Bend left at 6,700 feet to climb southwest through thickening growth. The last mile gets increasingly brushy, and some bushwhacking is necessary for the final stretch up the ridge to the summit.

A partly open view can be gained from 7,500-foot Mount Glenn. A ridge point a hundred yards northwest appears to be as high as the designated summit point.

There is a suggested route that avoids the difficult crossing of Carlink Canyon. Pick up road 795 leading northwest from road 84 only six miles west of Sunsites. Drive two miles northwest into the national forest and bear left to park south of Blacktail Hill. Hike south in order to gain an east ridge. Turn right on the ridge and climb to the 6,700-foot level. Join the route previously described.

■

46

Mount Ballard

General description: An off-trail ridge ascent
Hiking distance: 3 miles
Starting elevation: 6,020 feet
High point: 7,370 feet
Elevation gain: 1,500 feet
Map: 7.5 minute Bisbee

T he Mule Mountains are a small range near the
Mexican border. The mountains surround the town
of Bisbee and a main highway traverses the heart of
the range. Mount Ballard is the high point of the Mule
Mountains. The hike is short since you can start at a
high elevation just off the highway.

From US 80 in the northern part of Bisbee, drive to
Mule Pass. The pass is on a side road that is above a
highway tunnel. Park in the large parking area at
6,020-foot Mule Pass.
The hiking route from Mule Pass is along the ridge
running southwest to Mount Ballard. Most of the ridge
and the summit area of Mount Ballard is on Bureau of
Land Management land. While there is no constructed
trail, you can follow beaten paths much of the way.
Part of the time you are following a fence line. Large
bushes and trees often block the way, but careful
maneuvering usually gets you through without too

much trouble. There are several minor ridge points to be crossed, which interrupt the gradual ascent.

There are good views from Mount Ballard, which at 7,370 feet is only a little higher than several other points in the area. Mount Martin, also above seven thousand feet, is southeast. Northeast across the highway are other high points. Fissure Peak, a ridge point of 7,340 feet, almost as high as Mount Ballard, is northwest along the ridge only a half mile away.

For a little added exercise, you can follow the ridge northwest to Fissure Peak. Return the way you came.

■

47

Swisshelm Mountain

Swisshelm Mountain.

General description: An off-trail hike through open country
with a little bushwhacking and rock scrambling
Hiking distance: 5 miles
Starting elevation: 5,700 feet
High point: 7,185 feet
Elevation gain: 2,000 feet
Map: 7.5 minute Swisshelm Mountain (essential)

■

T he Swisshelm Mountains are a small range dwarfed
   by the Chiricahua Mountains to the northeast. The
Swisshelm Mountains are mostly barren of trees and
have scattered brush cover. The highest portion of the
mountains is on Bureau of Land Management land.
The high point and only named summit has the same
name as the range, Swisshelm Mountain. The
Swisshelm Mountains were named for John Swisshelm,
who prospected in the area in the 1870s. The climb to
Swisshelm Mountain is short and relatively easy
off-trail hiking in open country.

   Drive on US 666 between Interstate 10 and Douglas.
Eight miles south of the junction with Arizona 181,
turn east on a secondary road. Drive nine miles east to
a junction, take the right fork, and drive three miles
southeast to a side road leading south to the right.
This side road leaves the main road where the main
road makes a sharp turn to the left. Drive south on the
side road, staying with the most prominent road for
three and a half miles. Take the left fork at a junction
and drive south up a canyon past some mine properties
for another two miles. Park in a level area at 5,700 feet,
just before the road descends into a broad canyon.
   The entry road crosses a patchwork of state, BLM,
and private lands. The last portion of this trip may be
too rough for passenger cars, so you may need to park
sooner. Be careful to obey any restrictions on parking
or entry.
   Hike southwest up the open ridge, staying right of a
canyon. At an elevation of 6,700 feet, circle left around
the head of the canyon and gain the ridge crest. Here
you are in a saddle south of a 6,982-foot ridge point.
Continue south and southeast along the ridge, climbing

over several ridge points. You finally stroll along a broad 6,820-foot saddle and make the final climb southeast to the summit.

At the summit with its benchmark, you get an appealing view of the green Chiricahua Mountains to the northeast. Northwest across the valley you can see the rugged spires of the Dragoon Mountains.

■

48

Dos Cabezas Peaks

Dos Cabezas Peaks.

General description: A short off-trail hike followed by a
   stiff climb with bushwhacking and rock scrambling
Hiking distance: 3 miles
Starting elevation: 7,220 feet
High point: 8,354 feet
Elevation gain: 1,500 feet
Map: 7.5 minute Dos Cabezas

•

T he Dos Cabezas Mountains are a northwestern extension of the Chiricahua Mountains. The Dos Cabezas Mountains are not nearly as heavily wooded as the Chiricahua Mountains. The high points of the range are the Dos Cabezas Peaks. The plural is used because there are two summits of almost equal height. You will need to climb both of them to be sure of getting to the high point.

Drive southeast from Willcox on Arizona 186 to the small town of Dos Cabezas. Turn north and drive the road that goes up Mascot Canyon. Stay right at a fork after two miles, pass a side road on the right in another quarter mile, and turn right at a "T" after another mile. Drive east a quarter mile and then make a sharp turn left to wind northwest up the hill. Another mile or so of driving brings you to the range crest at 7,220 feet. Here you are just west of a radio facility. The drive to the range crest may require a high clearance vehicle, so you might have to add some more walking distance to this short hike. The road from the highway to the range crest goes through a maze of private, state, and Bureau of Land Management land. The summits are on BLM land.

Walk west along the range crest over a small hill to another saddle of 7,220 feet. Then climb more steeply west to a radio facility on a 7,900-foot ridge point. Follow the mostly level ridge northwest to the base of the southernmost of the two summits. The climb is directly up the cliffs to the high point. It is necessary to search out a best route by weaving between the steeper cliff faces. We found that a route from left to right and back to the left again works well. Some climbers have been able to locate a walk-up route, but

The north summit from the south summit, Dos Cabezas Peaks.

we didn't find one. Others may prefer to just scramble up the rocky cliff faces instead of looking for an easier route.

When you reach the south summit, you can puzzle on whether or not it is higher than the north summit. Each summit has three forty-foot contours above the 8,200-foot contour on the topographic map. The northern summit has a listed elevation of 8,354 feet. The southern summit has no listed elevation and would interpolate to 8,340 feet, but it could be as high as 8,359 feet. Regardless of its elevation, the southern summit gives fantastic views in all directions.

The hardest part of getting from the southern summit to the northern one is the descent to the saddle between the two summits. There are several very steep gullies that could be used for the descent. We used the central one that runs somewhat from left to right. Some climbers may want the protection of a belay or may want to rappel down this stretch. Once in the saddle between the two summits at 8,180 feet, it is no problem to scramble north to the northern summit. After looking carefully from each summit, there may still be disagreement in your party as to which summit is higher.

Return to the saddle between the two summits. Unless you particularly want to go over the south summit again, you can avoid it by descending to the east. Contour southeast as you descend through the timber to reach a vehicle track that leads to the saddle east of the radio facility. Now on your previous route, proceed east over the small knoll back to the point where you first came up to the ridge crest.

■

49

Flys Peak; Peak 9,570; Chiricahua Peak; Snowshed Peak; Paint Rock; Raspberry Peak; and Monte Vista Peak

Chiricahua Peak.

General description: A long trail hike with some off-trail climbing in the woods and a short rock scramble
Hiking distance: 22 miles
Starting elevation: 8,460 feet
High point: 9,759 feet
Elevation gain: 6,000 feet
Maps: 7.5 minute Rustler Park;
7.5 minute Chiricahua Peak (essential);
Coronado National Forest (Chiricahua Mountains)

.

T he Chiricahua Mountains are Arizona's most
southeasterly mountain range. The outstanding
network of trails makes this beautiful country excellent
for hiking and backpacking. Seven summits of the
Chiricahuas pierce the nine-thousand-foot level, topped
by Chiricahua Peak at 9,759 feet. The Chiricahua
Wilderness encompasses much of the range.

The seven high points of the Chiricahuas can be
visited on one big day hike, but this may not allow
enough time for many people to savor the beauties of
this magnificent mountain range. Alternatives are to
take the trip described here as a two- or three-day
backpack, or to approach the peaks on several different
day hikes.

To climb all seven summits on one day hike or a
backpack, the best starting point is Rustler Park. This
trailhead, at an elevation of 8,460 feet, gives you a
chance to visit the summits by using the trails along
the crest of the range.

Drive southeast from Interstate 10 on Arizona 186 or
US 666 and Arizona 181 toward Chiricahua National
Monument. After driving east toward the monument
three miles from the junction of Arizona 186 and 181,
turn south on forest road 42. Follow road 42 as it
climbs southeasterly to the crest of the range at Onion
Saddle. An eastern approach to Onion Saddle is off of
US 80 through Portal. At Onion Saddle, drive south on
forest road 42D to Rustler Park Campground. With a
high clearance vehicle, sometimes some hiking distance
can be saved by driving on past Rustler Park
Campground to the end of the road near Long Park.

If you start hiking at Rustler Park, hike west on a
trail that joins the Crest Trail. Turn left and hike south

on the Crest Trail past Bootlegger Saddle, through
Long Park, and to a trail junction at a 9,020-foot saddle
in Flys Park. The trail from the road end at Long Park
joins the Crest Trail at Flys Park. Take the left-forking
trail at Flys Park and climb steeply to 9,667-foot Flys
Peak. The trail goes over the west side of the summit,
with a short spur trail leading to the top. There is little
view from the summit, but there is a good view point
at some rocky cliffs southeast of the high point.

Return west off the summit of Flys Peak and pick up
the main trail going south. Descend steeply on the trail
to a 9,247-foot saddle at Round Park. Peak 9,570, the
only unnamed summit above nine thousand feet in the
Chiricahuas, is south of Round Park. The trail rounds
this summit on its east side, but there is no trail to the
top. Leave the trail on the right soon after passing
Round Park and head south through the timber to the
high point. There is no view. You can return to the trail
the way you came. In this case, turn right and follow
the trail around the east side of Peak 9,570 to a
junction at Cima Park. With a good sense of direction,
it is possible to descend southeast or south off of Peak
9,570 to meet the trail at or near the junction in Cima
Park.

Take the trail going south from Cima Park and then
choose the left fork in a quarter mile and walk to
Junction Saddle on the north side of Chiricahua Peak.
Just beyond Junction Saddle, turn right at a trail
junction and hike up the trail to Chiricahua Peak. This
high point of the Chiricahua Mountains at 9,759 feet
offers no view.

Continue on the trail over Chiricahua Peak toward
the next objective, Snowshed Peak. The route descends
through a saddle, contours left around the north side
of a ridge point, and then climbs on the left (east) fork
from another trail junction. The trail climbs east to the

Paint Rock.

9,665-foot summit. The views are much better on the way up than they are from the top.

Return toward Chiricahua Peak but this time take the left-forking (west) trail at the peak's southeast flank. This trail leads to Chiricahua Saddle on the southwest side of Chiricahua Peak. Turn left at the trail junction in the saddle and hike south on the Crest Trail.

Paint Rock is a mile south of Chiricahua Saddle. The Crest Trail climbs steeply and rounds the right side of some impressive cliffs. Just beyond the cliffs you are a little south of the 9,375-foot high point of Paint Rock. The off-trail climb to Paint Rock is steep and takes a little rock scrambling. Leave the trail on the right and pick a route up between steep rock formations. Scramble up through some minor cliff bands to find your way to the highest rock. The view from this point is superlative, the best view we've found in the Chiricahua Mountains other than from a lookout tower. We always like to eat lunch at a place with a view, and Paint Rock is a choice lunch spot for this long hike.

From Paint Rock, return to the trail and proceed south less than a mile to a trail junction north of Raspberry Peak. Don't take either fork, but climb south between the two trails through the timber to the top of Raspberry Peak. Raspberry Peak, a 9,420-foot summit, is said to be named for the large amount of raspberries on its western slope. Unfortunately, we weren't there when the raspberries were ripe. You can look for raspberries on the way down since the route leads down the western slope of the mountain to meet the trail.

Pick up the trail at a 9,220-foot saddle west of Raspberry Peak and follow the trail on west. The next objective is Monte Vista Peak, a 9,355-foot named point with a lookout tower. Find a short spur trail on the eastern slope of Monte Vista Peak and follow it to the summit. The lookout tower provides outstanding views.

After climbing the seven summits, return by following the trails back past Raspberry Peak and Paint Rock to Chiricahua Saddle. Take a trail that skirts the west side of Chiricahua Peak to Junction Saddle. Follow the Crest Trail north to Cima Park, Round Park and Flys Park. This trail enables you to skirt Peak 9,570 on the east and Flys Peak on the west. At Flys Park, take a trail either to Rustler Park or Long Park to return to your starting point.

For those who would rather hike than drive to the range crest, Turkey Creek makes a good starting point. The trailheads in Turkey Creek are at or below 6,600 feet compared with 8,460 feet at Rustler Park. The Morman Ridge Trail, the Morse Canyon Trail, and the Pole Bridge Canyon Trail make reasonable approaches from Turkey Creek to the high peaks. Two of the three trails can be combined with the Crest Trail for a good loop trip.

Just as we were completing this manuscript, we have received information that there may be two more nine-thousand-foot named points in the Chiricahuas. A preliminary map shows Sentinel Peak, southeast of Snowshed Peak, to be a nine-thousander, instead of 8,999 feet shown on the old 15 minute map. In addition, a 9,010-foot point just northwest of Sentinel Peak is named "Finnicum Peak." So changes in the list of high summits can be expected as more accurate mapping and naming of high points continues.

■

Arizona's Highest Summits
Excluding Those on Indian Reservations

.

Rank	Elev.	Name of the Summit	Mountain Range	Location	Topographic Map
1	12,633	Humphreys Peak	San Francisco	Coconino NF	Humphreys Peak
2	12,356	Agassiz Peak	San Francisco	Coconino NF	Humphreys Peak
3	11,969	Fremont Peak	San Francisco	Coconino NF	Humphreys Peak
	11,838	Aubineau Peak	San Francisco	Coconino NF	Humphreys Peak
	11,474	Rees Peak	San Francisco	Coconino NF	Humphreys Peak
4	11,460	Doyle Peak	San Francisco	Coconino NF	Humphreys Peak
5	11,420	Mount Baldy	White	Apache NF	Mount Baldy
6	10,912	Escudilla Mountain	White	Apache NF	Alpine 15'
7	10,720	Mount Graham	Pinaleno	Coronado NF	Mount Graham
	10,627	Hawk Peak	Pinaleno	Coronado NF	Webb Peak
8	10,418	Kendrick Peak	——	Kaibab NF	Kendrick Peak
	10,370	Plain View Peak	Pinaleno	Coronado NF	Mount Graham
9	10,133	Greens Peak	White	Apache NF	Greens Peak
10	10,092	(Thick Top)	White	Apache NF	Alpine 15'
	10,083	Schultz Peak	San Francisco	Coconino NF	Humphreys Peak
11	10,030	Webb Peak	Pinaleno	Coronado NF	Webb Peak
12	10,022	Heliograph Peak	Pinaleno	Coronado NF	Mount Graham
13	9,947	unnamed: SE of Greens Peak	White	Apache NF	Greens Peak
14	9,913	unnamed: S of Greens Peak	White	Apache NF	Greens Peak
15	9,910	(Grassy Top)	White	Apache NF	Greens Peak
16	9,880	(Burro Mountain)	White	Apache NF	Big Lake 15'
17	9,793	Pole Knoll	White	Apache NF	Greens Peak
18	9,764	Wahl Knoll	White	Apache NF	Big Lake 15'

Rank	Elev.	Name of the Summit	Mountain Range	Location	Topographic Map
19	9,759	Chiricahua Peak	Chiricahua	Coronado NF	Chiricahua Peak
20	9,667	Flys Peak	Chiricahua	Coronado NF	Chiricahua Peak
21	9,665	Snowshed Peak	Chiricahua	Coronado NF	Chiricahua Peak
22	9,660	Grand View Peak	Pinaleno	Coronado NF	Webb Peak
23	9,651	Pat Knoll	White	Apache NF	Big Lake 15'
24	9,636	Saint Peters Dome	White	Apache NF	Whiting Knoll
25	9,585	(Noble View Peak)	White	Apache NF	Alpine 15'
26	9,570	unnamed: S of Flys Peak	Chiricahua	Coronado NF	Chiricahua Peak
27	9,560	(Flat Top)	White	Apache NF	Alpine 15'
	9,560	Rudd Knoll	White	Apache NF	Big Lake 15'
28	9,559	unnamed: W of Greens Peak	White	Apache NF	Greens Peak
29	9,524	Boardshack Knoll	White	Apache NF	Mount Baldy
30	9,507	unnamed: NW of Noble Mtn.	White	Apache NF	Alpine 15'
31	9,480	(High Point)	White	Apache NF	Hannagan Meadow 15'
	9,480	Noble Mountain	White	Apache NF	Alpine 15'
32	9,477	Grant Hill	Pinaleno	Coronado NF	Webb Peak
33	9,466	Miller Peak	Huachuca	Coronado NF	Miller Peak
	9,464	Pool Knoll	White	Apache NF	Big Lake 15'
34	9,453	Mount Wrightson	Santa Rita	Coronado NF	Mount Wrightson
	9,424	Sizer Knoll	White	Apache NF	Greer
35	9,420	Raspberry Peak	Chiricahua	Coronado NF	Chiricahua Peak
36	9,419	S U Knolls	White	Apache NF	Big Lake 15'
37	9,415	Big Lake Knoll	White	Apache NF	Big Lake 15'
38	9,400	unnamed: N of Hannagan Mdw.	White	Apache NF	Hannagan Meadow 15'
39	9,400	(Timber Top)	White	Apache NF	Alpine 15'
40	9,388	Sitgreaves Mountain	——	Kaibab NF	Williams 15'
41	9,387	unnamed: SW of Whiting Knoll	White	Apache NF	Whiting Knoll
	9,380	Eagle Rock	Pinaleno	Coronado NF	Mount Graham
	9,375	Paint Rock	Chiricahua	Coronado NF	Chiricahua Peak
	9,355	Monte Vista Peak	Chiricahua	Coronado NF	Chiricahua Peak
42	9,348	Whiting Knoll	White	Apache NF	Whiting Knoll

Arizona's Highest Summits

Rank	Elev.	Name of the Summit	Mountain Range	Location	Topographic Map
43	9,346	Blue Peak	White	Apache NF	Hannagan Meadow 15'
44	9,320	(Tank Top)	White	Apache NF	Big Lake 15'
45	9,320	unnamed: SE of Big Lake	White	Apache NF	Big Lake 15'
46	9,299	Elden Mountain	——	Coconino NF	Flagstaff East
	9,288	Merrill Peak	Pinaleno	Coronado NF	Webb Peak
47	9,283	Sugarloaf	San Francisco	Coconino NF	Sunset Crater West
48	9,256	Bill Williams Mountain	——	Kaibab NF	Bill Williams Mountain 15'
49	9,254	unnamed: SW of Escudilla Mtn.	White	Apache NF	Alpine 15'
50	9,240	unnamed: SW of Kaibab Lodge	Kaibab Plateau	Kaibab NF	De Motte Park 15'
51	9,240	unnamed: NW of S Canyon Sp.	Kaibab Plateau	Kaibab NF	De Motte Park 15'
52	9,237	Carr Peak	Huachuca	Coronado NF	Miller Peak
53	9,185	unnamed: NE of Escudilla Mtn.	White	Apache NF	Alpine 15'
	9,184	Salt benchmark	White	Apache NF	Hannagan Meadow 15'
54	9,170	Hochderffer Hills	——	Coconino NF	Kendrick Peak
55	9,157	Mount Lemmon	Santa Catalina	Coronado NF	Mount Lemmon
56	9,146	(Mount Ian)	Santa Rita	Coronado NF	Mount Wrightson
57	9,143	(Turner View)	White	Apache NF	Alpine 15'
58	9,121	(Renos Neighbor)	White	Apache NF	Hannagan Meadow 15'
	9,094	Reno Lookout	White	Apache NF	Hannagan Meadow 15'
59	9,080	(Valley View Peak)	White	Apache NF	Alpine 15'
60	9,071	unnamed: NE of Escudilla Mtn.	White	Apache NF	Alpine 15'
61	9,069	Loco Knoll	White	Apache NF	Loco Knoll
62	9,065	White Horse Hills	——	Coconino NF	White Horse Hills
	9,058	Tenney Mountain	White	Apache NF	Alpine 15'
	9,018	Little Elden Mountain	——	Coconino NF	Sunset Crater West
	9,006	Clark Peak	Pinaleno	Coronado NF	Webb Peak
63	9,004	unnamed: E of Sitgreaves Mtn.	——	Kaibab NF	Parks
64	9,003	Antelope Mountain	White	state land	Greer
65	9,000	(Alpine View Peak)	White	Apache NF	Alpine 15'
66	9,000	unnamed: N of Alpine Divide	White	Apache NF	Alpine 15'

Notes

Ranked summits rise at least three hundred feet above all saddles connecting them with higher mountains.

Named high points that do not rise three hundred feet above all saddles connecting to higher mountains are listed but not ranked.

Topographic maps are 7.5 minute except where otherwise indicated.

Names in parentheses are unofficial.

■

High Points
of Selected Mountain Ranges
Between Seven Thousand and Nine Thousand Feet

.

Rank	Elev.	Name of the Mountain	Mountain Range	Location	7.5 Minute Map
1	8,664	Mica Mountain	Rincon	Saguaro NM	Mica Mountain
2	8,417	Hualapai Peak	Hualapai	County Park	Hualapai Peak
3	8,354	Dos Cabezas Peaks	Dos Cabezas	BLM	Dos Cabezas
4	7,979	Mount Union	Bradshaw	Prescott NF	Groom Creek
5	7,903	Mazatzal Peak	Mazatzal	Tonto NF	Mazatzal Peak
6	7,848	Pinal Peak	Pinal	Tonto NF	Pinal Peak
7	7,748	Aztec Peak	Sierra Ancha	Tonto NF	Aztec Peak
8	7,734	Baboquivari Peak	Baboquivari	BLM	Baboquivari Peak
9	7,711	Apache Peak	Whetstone	Coronado NF	Apache Peak
10	7,663	Bassett Peak	Galiuro	Coronado NF	Bassett Peak
11	7,631	Reiley Peak	Winchester	Coronado NF	Reiley Peak
12	7,626	Granite Mountain	Granite	Prescott NF	Jerome Canyon
13	7,550	Pinnacle Ridge	Santa Teresa	Coronado NF	Buford Hill
14	7,500	Mount Glenn	Dragoon	Coronado NF	Cochise Stronghold
15	7,370	Mount Ballard	Mule	BLM	Bisbee
16	7,270	Hyde Creek Mountain	Santa Maria	Prescott NF	Camp Wood
17	7,221	Mount Washington	Patagonia	Coronado NF	Duquesne
18	7,185	Swisshelm Mountain	Swisshelm	BLM	Swisshelm Mountains
19	7,100	Juniper Mesa	Juniper	Prescott NF	Juniper Mountains

■

Appendix Three

Arizona's Highest Summits on Indian Reservations

.

Rank	Elev.	Name of the Summit	Mountain Range	Reservation	7.5 Minute Map
	11,403	Baldy Peak	White	Fort Apache	Mount Baldy
1	11,357	Mount Ord	White	Fort Apache	Mount Baldy
2	11,150	Paradise Butte	White	Fort Apache	Mount Baldy
	11,036	Mount Warren	White	Fort Apache	Mount Baldy
3	10,932	*unnamed*: N of Mount Baldy	White	Fort Apache	Mount Baldy
4	10,624	Diamond Butte	White	Fort Apache	Hawley Lake East
5	10,365	*unnamed*: SW of Mount Baldy	White	Fort Apache	Mount Baldy
	10,346	Spruce Mountain	White	Fort Apache	Hawley Lake East
	10,185	Tiger Butte	White	Fort Apache	Hawley Lake East
6	9,970	Burnt Mountain	White	Fort Apache	Bonito Rock
7	9,820	Roof Butte	Chuska	Navajo	Roof Butte
8	9,778	*unnamed*: NW of Roof Butte	Chuska	Navajo	Roof Butte
9	9,773	Apache Butte	White	Fort Apache	Hawley Lake East
10	9,658	*unnamed*: W of Roof Butte	Chuska	Navajo	Roof Butte
11	9,646	*unnamed*: W of Tiger Butte	White	Fort Apache	Hawley Lake East
12	9,643	*unnamed*: SW of Greens Peak	White	Fort Apache	Greens Peak
13	9,635	Big Cienega Mountain	White	Fort Apache	Greens Peak
14	9,566	*unnamed*: SE of Roof Butte	Chuska	Navajo	Roof Butte
15	9,550	Matthews Peak	Tunitcha	Navajo	Tsaile
16	9,466	*unnamed*: S of View Point	Lukachukia	Navajo	Cove
17	9,460	*unnamed*	Lukachukia	Navajo	Lukachukia
18	9,420	*unnamed*: SE of Matthews Pk.	Tunitcha	Navajo	Tsaile Butte
19	9,407	Pastora Peak	Carrizo	Navajo	Pastora Peak

Arizona's Highest Summits on Indian Reservations

Rank	Elev.	Name of the Summit	Mountain Range	Reservation	7.5 Minute Map
20	9,368	*unnamed*: N of Zibetod Peak	Carrizo	Navajo	Pastora Peak
21	9,308	Soldier Butte	White	Fort Apache	Horseshoe Cienega
22	9,300	*unnamed*: W of Roof Butte	Chuska	Navajo	Lukachukia
	9,300	Zibetod Peak	Carrizo	Navajo	Pastora Peak
23	9,285	*unnamed*: SE of Roof Butte	Chuska	Navajo	Roof Butte
24	9,269	*unnamed*: W of Roof Butte	Chuska	Navajo	Lukachukia
25	9,263	Boundary Butte	White	Fort Apache	Boundary Butte
26	9,251	Corral benchmark	Carrizo	Navajo	Pastora Peak
27	9,249	*unnamed*: S of Roof Butte	Tunitcha	Navajo	Roof Butte
28	9,246	*unnamed*: S of Roof Butte	Tunitcha	Navajo	Roof Butte
29	9,242	*unnamed*	White	Fort Apache	Hawley Lake East
30	9,215	Aspen Butte	White	Fort Apache	Bonito Rock
31	9,203	*unnamed*: NW of Soldier Butte	White	Fort Apache	Horseshoe Cienega
32	9,198	*unnamed*: E of Matthews Peak	Tunitcha	Navajo	Tsaile Butte
33	9,182	Tsaile Peak	Tunitcha	Navajo	Tsaile Butte
34	9,180	*unnamed*: E of Matthews Peak	Tunitcha	Navajo	Tsaile Butte
35	9,175	McKays Peak	White	Fort Apache	Hawley Lake West
36	9,161	Cerro Gordo Mountain	White	Fort Apache	Boundary Butte
37	9,119	*unnamed*: W of Apache Butte	White	Fort Apache	Hawley Lake East
38	9,110	Cinder Pit Mountain	White	Fort Apache	Horseshoe Cienega
39	9,108	View Point	Lukachukia	Navajo	Cove
40	9,082	*unnamed*: N of Tsaile Peak	Tunitcha	Navajo	Tsaile Butte
41	9,062	*unnamed*: W of Soldier Butte	White	Fort Apache	Horseshoe Cienega
42	9,060	*unnamed*: S of Bear benchmark	Tunitcha	Navajo	Tsaile Butte
43	9,059	*unnamed*: E of White Cone	Chuska	Navajo	Upper Wheatfields
44	9,020	*unnamed*: SE of Matthews Peak	Chuska	Navajo	Tsaile Butte

Index

.

N

O

P

R

Raspberry Peak, 158-163
Rees Peak, 38-40
Reiley Canyon, 118
Reiley Peak, 117-118
Reno Lookout, 105-108
Renos Neighbor, 105-108
Riggs Lake, 124
Riggs Ranch, 131

Rincon Mountain Wilderness, 128
Rincon Mountains, 128
Romero Pass, 127
Round Park, 160
Rudd Knoll, 77-81
Rustler Park, 159-163
Rustler Park Campground, 159

S

S U Knolls, 86-89
Safford, 113, 120
Saguaro National Monument, 128-129
Saint Peters Dome, 68-69
Salt benchmark, 105-108
San Francisco Mountain
    11, 18, 20, 23, 26, 31, 41-42
Sandy Saddle, 58
Santa Catalina Mountains, 126-127
Santa Maria Mountains, 50, 54
Santa Rita Mountains, 135-137
Santa Teresa Mountains, 113
Santa Teresa Wilderness, 113-114
Schultz Pass, 31, 34, 41
Schultz Pass Road, 31, 41
Schultz Peak, 33-35
Schultz Tank, 31
Sentinel Peak, 163
Shake Tree Trail, 58-59
Shannon Campground, 120-121
Sheep Crossing, 84-85

Sierra Ancha Mountains, 62
Sierra Ancha Wilderness, 62
Sierra Vista, 142
Signal Peak, 64
Silver Range, 55
Sitgreaves Mountain, 18-21
Sizer Knoll, 77-81
Snow Bowl, 25-26, 28-29
Snowshed Peak, 158-163
South Canyon Spring, 44
Springerville, 68, 71, 87, 91
Stockton Hill Road, 14
Sugarloaf, 36-37
Suicide Ridge, 59
Sunset Crater National Monument
    36, 42
Sunsites, 147-148
Super Trail, 137
Swift Trail, 124
Swisshelm, John, 152
Swisshelm Mountain, 151-153

T

Tank Top, 86-89
Tanque Verde Mountains, 129
Tanque Verde Peak, 129
Tanque Verde Road, 126
Tenney Mountain, 102-104
Terry Flat, 94, 96-97

Thick Top, 96-97
Thomas Canyon, 131-132
Three Points, 131
Timber Top, 102-104
Tohono O'odham Indian Reservation
    134

Index

Tonto National Forest, 45, 62, 64
Toolbox Draw, 94
Tucson, 126

Turkey Creek, 162
Turner Peak, 92
Turner View, 90-92

U

Union, (Mount), 55-56

V

Valley View Peak, 98-101

W

Wahl Knoll, 77-81
Walnut Creek, 47
Washington, (Mount), 138-140
Webb Peak, 123-125
West Fork Little Colorado River, 82, 84
Whetstone Mountains, 144-146
White Horse Hills, 24-26
White Mountain Reservoir, 75

White Mountains, 67-109
Whiting Knoll, 68-69
Willcox, 115, 117, 155
Williamson Valley Road, 47, 50
Winchester Mountains, 117
Workman Creek Falls, 62-63
Wrightson, (Mount), 135-137

■

About the Authors

.

B ob and Dotty Martin have hiked together in
Arizona since beginning to spend their winters
there in 1979. They are also co-authors of *Hiking
Guide to the Santa Rita Mountains of Arizona.*

Summers find the Martins in Colorado, where Bob
has authored *Hiking the Highest Passes* and *Hiking Trails
of Central Colorado* and co-authored *Colorado's High
Thirteeners.*

Bob and Dotty met over forty years ago in a
university orchestra and continue to play chamber
music together.

Other Outdoor Books by Cordillera Press

.

Take 'em Along: Sharing the Wilderness with Your Children
By Barbara J. Euser

128 pp., 45 Photos, (5½ x 8½), ISBN: 0-917895-12-6, $11.95, Softcover.

The Outdoor Athlete: Total Training for Outdoor Performance
By Steve Ilg

288 pp., Photos, Illustrations, (6 x 9), ISBN: 0-917895-17-7, $12.95, Softcover.

The San Juan Mountains: A Climbing and Hiking Guide
By Robert F. Rosebrough

274 pp., Photos, Maps, (5½ x 8½), ISBN: 0-917895-07-X, $12.95, Softcover.

Roof of the Rockies: A History of Colorado Mountaineering
By William M. Bueler

264 pp., Photos, Maps, (5½ x 8½), ISBN: 0-917895-06-1, $12.95, Softcover.

Colorado's High Thirteeners: A Climbing and Hiking Guide
By Mike Garratt and Bob Martin

260 pp., Photos, Charts, (5½ x 8½), ISBN: 0-917895-03-7, $11.95, Softcover.

Cordillera Press
Post Office Box 3699
Evergreen, Colorado 80439
303 / 670-3010